TORI
AMOS
IN THE STUDIO

JAKE BROWN

GW01003624

ECW PRESS

Copyright © Jake Brown, 2011

Published by ECW Press
2120 Queen Street East, Suite 200, Toronto, Ontario, Canada M4E 1E2
416-694-3348 / info@ecwpress.com

All rights reserved. No part of this publication may be reproduced, stored in a retrieval system, or transmitted in any form by any process — electronic, mechanical, photocopying, recording, or otherwise — without the prior written permission of the copyright owners and ECW Press. The scanning, uploading, and distribution of this book via the Internet or via any other means without the permission of the publisher is illegal and punishable by law. Please purchase only authorized electronic editions, and do not participate in or encourage electronic piracy of copyrighted materials. Your support of the author's rights is appreciated.

Tori Amos: In the Studio is not authorized or endorsed by Tori Amos, her management or representation.

LIBRARY AND ARCHIVES CANADA CATALOGUING IN PUBLICATION

Brown, Jake
Tori Amos : in the studio / Jake Brown.

ISBN 978-1-55022-945-5
ALSO ISSUED AS:
978-1-55490-945-2 (PDF); 978-1-55490-970-4 (EPUB)

1. Amos, Tori. 2. Rock musicians—United States—Biography.
I. Title.

ML420.A586B878 2011   782.42166'092   C2011-900666-9

Editor: Crissy Boylan
Cover and text design: Tania Craan
Typesetting: Troy Cunningham
Printing: Friesens 1 2 3 4 5

MIX
Paper from
responsible sources
FSC
www.fsc.org   FSC® C016245

Photo credits: front cover © Frederic Dugit/Maxppp/Landov; back cover © Reuters/Lucas Jackson/Landov; page 4 © Dave Allocca/Retna; page 42 © Jay Blakesberg; page 76 © Michel Linssen/Redferns/Getty Images; pages 110 and 113 © James Cumpsty; page 124 © Jeffrey Millman; page 134 © Grant Scott/Camera Press/Retna; page 148 © David Atlas/Retna; page 160 © Lawrence/Starface/Retna. All album covers © their respective owners.

PRINTED AND BOUND IN CANADA

ECW PRESS
ecwpress.com

To my aunt Heather and my dear friend Helen Watts,
two shining examples of the kind of strong women
Tori has spent the last 20 years singing for

Table of Contents

"All the church hymns were coming through one ear, and The Beatles were coming through the other. I thought that if these are my two choices in life, then I definitely want what's behind door number two."

— TORI AMOS (*TIME OUT*, 1994)

CHAPTER 1

Those Formative Years

According to the Reverend Dr. Edison Amos, Methodist minister and father to the woman now known by millions of music enthusiasts as just "Tori," at five years old Myra Ellen Amos was already well on her way to becoming "a twenty-first century Mozart." Born August 22, 1963, to the Reverend Dr. and Mary Ellen Amos in the small city of Newton, North Carolina, little Myra didn't take long to reveal her gift for music. "[My mother] says I played music before I could talk," said Tori Amos, who lived with her family in Washington state and later the Baltimore, Maryland, area.

The former child prodigy — who calls music her first language, not English — shared some of her earliest impressions of the instrument that would come to be such an integral part of her life and career with *Performing Songwriter* in 2006: "In my dad's study, where he would write his sermon, there was a big black upright [piano] that somebody in the church had given my family. I remember crawling up onto this windy stool — you could wind it and it would get taller — and I would barely reach the keys. I remember feeling that this was my antenna to the galaxy, that I could cross dimensions through sound and hear back

from the outer reaches of the universe. . . . The songs were alive to me, as alive as the human beings around me that weren't making a whole lot of sense. But the songs were making sense."

Her childhood perspective on the piano was that of friendship and love, and she told *Rolling Stone* in 2002, "I knew I was a musician before I was potty-trained. I just always remember playing the piano." From the age of two-and-a-half, Tori was playing the piano and considered it her "best friend in the world. That was the only thing that understood me and that I understood. . . . When you're young, you're being told what to think. But I'd go to the piano and that's where I was comforted. It was my protector, the protector of my thoughts." In music, Tori found a sanctuary of sorts as well as an identity: "I knew I was a musician before I knew I was a girl. You know if you are a musician because I think music chooses you in some way. It's very hard to say no to it — it just envelops you."

Her mother, Mary Ellen, saw the connection her daughter had to music. In an interview with the *Sunday Times Magazine*, Mary Ellen recalled, "Before Tori could even talk, she hummed. By the time she was two-and-a-half, she would walk over to the piano and copy exactly what her brother or sister had just been practicing. She used to get up in the morning before anyone else and play. The piano was her playmate, and she could reproduce anything she heard by ear, songs on the radio or even entire scores." Tori was known as the little girl who played the piano; her innate musical ability shaped her identity as people always asked her to play for them. Her father said he wasn't "aware of [her talent] like the sun coming over the horizon, but we were noticing she would come in and play the piano right after [her brother and sister] had finished and it would sound a little better than them. But I think when we were astounded was when we took her to *Oliver!* or *The Sound of Music*. I'm not sure which one it was, and then after seeing that, she came in and sat down, and it seemed to me she could play the whole score."

Musical scores were among the first non-religious music Tori was exposed to. As she told the *Phoenix New Times* in 1998, "The shocking thing about *Oklahoma!* [is] it was the only thing I was allowed to play when I was little . . . I had all of this religious music I was learning, so I learned the soundtrack at a very young age." As if playing entire musical scores by ear wasn't enough, young Tori also began composing her own music and developing her vocal ability, singing what she wanted to communicate instead of simply talking. Still, while Amos's talent as a pianist evolved rapidly, she explained that, by contrast, her voice "came with age. I was no Shirley Temple. It took years and years to develop. Like you know how some little kids have great voices at first but get worse later? Well, I was the opposite. I vocally developed much later." Speaking to *iGuide* in 1996, Amos recalled an incident from school when she was just shy of 10 years old: "I was a really good piano player, but the teacher would have other girls sing while I played. When I tried to sing, I remember this one boy, Kevin Craig, wrote a note to a girl named Peggy and he said Ellen — which is what they called me — sings like a frog. The teacher read it in class in front of everybody, and I was never going to sing again. I had to develop my voice and I worked really, really hard developing it. The playing came easier at first."

From her earliest years, Tori spent her summers down in Newton, North Carolina, with her maternal grandparents, Calvin and Bertie Copeland. (It was on a trip back home to visit her family that Tori's mother gave birth to her; falling ill while there, her doctor advised Mary Ellen not to travel for the remainder of her pregnancy.) Tori's mother felt it was important that her daughter know about her Cherokee heritage and about the line of strong women she descended from. Amos's time spent with her grandparents shaped her, particularly by connecting her to her Eastern Cherokee heritage, an influence that would surface later in her music. Tales of her great-grandmother, Margaret Little, who "escaped the Trail of Tears and ran off into the Smoky Mountains in 1839" and who "married a plantation owner where she was a surrogate slave," and stories about the life of her people had been passed to Tori's grandfather, and he sang them to her. Michael, Amos's older brother, told the Raleigh, North Carolina, *News and Observer* in 1996 that "Tori really was the apple of my grandfather's eye. She was his last grandchild and came along after he had retired, so he spent a lot of time with her. I think she does get some of her musical ability from him."

Though her grandfather died when she was nine-and-a-half years old, his influence on her was lifelong. "I would sit on the porch with him," Amos told *Buffalo News* in 2003. "He'd smoke the sacred tobacco and tell me these stories. I don't think I realized at the time how profoundly he was changing me." The tradition of oral storytelling was passed down to the future songwriter by her grandfather who spent "a lot of time with me as a little kid, trying to explain to me about not needing to change another person to fit my own needs, and how that was breaking a deep spiritual law." Said Tori, "My grandfather made these memories come alive by telling me stories of his people. I felt an amazing sense of compassion toward what had happened to them, and I'm convinced that before he died, my grandfather hid a remember-the-stories chip underneath my skin."

In addition to fostering a love of storytelling, music, and creativity, Tori believes her grandfather "instilled in me [the idea] that spirit is in all things. I've always believed that. . . . It was a real natural way of looking at life." Speaking with *Newsday* in 2001, Tori explained, "He would try to teach me how to be a container for a different frequency that didn't seem to be your own. He would get frustrated with me because I would just want to watch *Scooby-Doo*, but he really had a huge impact on my life. Everything he tried to teach me, I didn't necessarily achieve it all, but he is like a tape recorder. I do remember. Sometimes I can hear him clear as a bell." On long walks together, Tori's grandfather would challenge her to look past the obvious: "He would ask me what I saw and usually I would describe whatever was right in front of me. And then he would make me ask questions: he would say, 'Well you're only looking at the surface of this.' He taught me how to study people, to listen to what they weren't saying. He really did want me to try and listen. He was my greatest teacher."

Her love and admiration for her maternal grandparents stands in sharp contrast to the influence her father's parents had on her. Tori once quipped that should she meet her paternal grandmother, Addie Allen, "at the River Styx, I don't know if I'd give her a ride in my boat."

Living deep in the Appalachian Mountains ("The Waltons looked like luxury compared to them"), both Addie and her husband were ordained ministers, which granted them authority in their community and a degree of power that, even from a young age, Tori felt was misused. "She was educated — it was almost unheard of in the 1920s for a woman to go to university — and she was very Christianized. I call her The Puritanical, The Shame Inducer. I was brought up in the city, outside Washington, but she lived six hours south, in the mountains. Have you seen the movie *Deliverance*? I knew those guys! I knew the pig!" Tori unabashedly told *She* in 1998: "From the age of five, I hated my grandmother. [She] believed that a young woman should turn her body over to her husband, who then owns it. Until then, she said, you should remain untouched. She told me that if I didn't love Jesus there would be no money for me in the Christmas kitty." While the rest of the family felt Addie was a "saint," young Tori felt she was the enemy. "She was an evil thing, no question. I'm sure I could have been the youngest child in jail for murdering my grandmother. At five, I wanted to take the butter knife and slit her throat," she said to *High Life* in 2001. "She and I were definitely on different peaks. She was full of self-righteousness and guilt and finger-pointing. It was very hard for my grandmother to claim the dark side of her femininity."

The dynamic within Amos's immediate family was less troubled. To *Seventeen* magazine, Tori related, "I had a great relationship with my sister. I have an older brother who is almost ten years older. My sister was seven years older. When I was seventeen, she was in medical school. She's just one of these people — I am just glad I got to know her as a sister, 'cause doctors can be very intimidating, but there's a really soft loving person there. She is brilliant medically, and because of that, she has helped to guide me." She describes her father as looking like James Dean, her mother as "very stylish" and as someone who had two distinct sides to her: "My mother's a southern lady, a sweetheart. She's definitely the minister's wife on one hand and then on the other she's a witch." Tori explains that her mother's non-traditional side is "a spirituality that goes beyond [Christianity]. She has premonitions and dreams, but she keeps her esoteric side to herself." Tori cites her mother's fortitude and compassion as qualities she hopes she inherited from her. Her life, in what she describes as a lower middle class family, was "a normal upbringing, in that way that I was the daughter of a Methodist minister and all the kids had to learn to play instruments at a very young age. I have never been sexually or in other physical ways abused. Sunday lunches after church. Going on vacation with the whole family. I've never been beaten. I don't have those kind of stories. I grew up and wanted to please everyone. Especially my dad. I wanted him to appreciate me and I was always wondering if I was doing my best, [working] hard enough."

While Tori's upbringing was nothing like the extreme stories of some child prodigies — the infamous tale of Beethoven's father beating him into deafness, for example — the Reverend Dr. Amos was "quite the disciplinarian when I was growing up," says the singer. As she explained to *Veronica* in 1994, "I could play the piano at three, and my father wanted me to go and play classical concerts, preferably all my life with the same orchestra." Her father began bringing the young pianist to weddings and funerals to perform; as she says, "I was cheaper than the organist." Tori tired of playing the same songs at every wedding and preferred funerals for the wider song selection.

"The one thing with being a child prodigy is you get so much attention," said Tori in 1994, "And when you're doing mini-recitals, you start to get addicted to approval. As a kid, I loved this restaurant [called] the Buttery, and when I did well, we'd go there. And when I did okay, we'd end up at Bob's Big Boy. Every time I played I knew it was about reward or not reward. That's kind of rough when you're six." Because of her extraordinary gift and perspective on the world, her childhood was far from ordinary, which was sometimes isolating. "I would get lonely sometimes when other children didn't want to come and play with me. I had millions of friends from the other [imaginary] world. As a little girl, you play with who you can, and if they're not in human form, they're still very real to you."

While she performed at church events where her father presided as reverend, Tori did not accept what she was being taught: "I was told what I was going to believe in rather than being told to develop my own belief system." For his part, Reverend Dr. Amos said in 1998, "I'd like to correct the misperception that Tori was reared in some sort of fire-and-brimstone fundamentalist tradition. We preach grace, mercy, and love. Tori was raised to be tolerant." (In other interviews, Tori has proudly mentioned that Reverend Amos marched with Martin Luther King Jr. in Washington, D.C., and was "very much part" of the civil rights movement.) Her mother, Mary Ellen, explained her perspective on Tori and her religious upbringing to the *Sunday Times Magazine*: "Tori questioned it all from the start, and we didn't really know how to answer her. She felt women were cheated in the church. I think she's wrong but I accept that God speaks to us all differently. Tori had an inquiring mind and was very outspoken, which got her into trouble. She spent a lot of time at school standing in the corner. Most of the time the congregation loved her, although she did some outlandish things. She was a wonderful choir director [when she was in her teens], but she used to come into church in red leather pants. She loved to shock and she still does. The young people in the choir would do anything for her, but some of the mothers didn't think too much of her. They made sarcastic remarks, which she hid from me. She'd come home and be wiping away the tears, and I didn't understand how cruel people were being."

While music in church (she was in the choir by age four) and scores to musicals were the earliest music Tori was exposed to, a broad range of music could be found in the Amos household as she grew up. "My brother had been plying me with all his records from the mid- to late-'60s, and my mother was trying to throw in her favorites from the '30s and '40s — Hoagy Carmichael and all that. I was being trained in the classics — Bartók, Debussy and the like." From Julie Andrews to Fats Waller to Gershwin to The Rolling Stones, Tori "would imitate everything." Her talent was developing too quickly for local music instructors, so her parents took up the church choir director's suggestion that they try the Peabody Institute, a music conservatory, in Baltimore. Mary Ellen recalled Tori's audition: "She played a selection from *Oliver!* and *The Sound of Music*. Then she played a classical piece and they started listening. They'd never taken anyone under nine, but they made an exception, and when they realized that on a clergyman's salary we couldn't afford it, they gave her a scholarship. The principal put her hand on my arm and said, 'God has given you the responsibility of raising this very rare child, and she has to be given every opportunity!'" From the perspective of young Tori, her parents' decision that she attend the Peabody was a little differently motivated, as she told Q in 1992: "When I was five, there was this Beatles album around the house, *Sgt. Pepper's*, and I was walking around with it, and my father said, 'What are you doing with it?' And I said, 'This is what I'm going to do.' My father went back to his paper with a look that said, 'She's out of her mind; she's going to the Peabody.'"

* * *

In 1968, Myra Ellen Amos became — and remains to date — the youngest student ever to enroll at the Peabody Institute, an internationally renowned conservatory and preparatory school, part of Johns Hopkins University in Baltimore. Tori remembers feeling excited that she'd be learning alongside older students; other than the five-year-old prodigy, the youngest student was nine years old, the rest were 16 and older. "The idea was to become a classical pianist," recalled Amos to *Keyboard* in 1992, "because what [else] are you going to do when you can play like that? . . . Wouldn't it be great for her to be around real musicians instead of just going to first grade?" Once enrolled at the Peabody, life for young Tori was unusual and she knew it: "My mother was reading me Edgar Allan Poe at night to help me go to sleep, then you go and read Dick and Jane and Spot [at school] and practice Mozart and Bartók in the afternoon [at the Peabody]. I was always writing music at my desk. It's not that I was that smart, but I was real creative."

Though Tori would remain studying at the Peabody until age 11, it was not without its difficulties. "I came in playing by ear and could play almost everything I heard. The whole idea was that to be a classical pianist you had to learn to read music. I knew that, but the way they did it was to try to break the ear so that it would force me to read." For a child whose relationship with the piano had been *play* in both senses of the word, it was an unwelcome change. "I was six and suddenly I was told there was a right and wrong way to play. For me, religion was about right and wrong. Methodism teaches you to restrict your emotions; music was my outlet. And when that freedom of expression became restricted it stopped being fun." Mary Ellen Amos could see that her daughter was struggling with reading music, as she told the *Sunday Times*: "She was in a group of students who were teenagers, and there she was, this little thing whose feet couldn't reach the pedals. Tori says the conservatory kicked her out. But what happened was that they cloned you to play in their classical way, and we could see her interest dwindling." In 1992, Tori spoke to the *Washington Post* about her experience at the Peabody: "They didn't know how to teach that kid. To try and break a kid's ear so that they'll learn how to read — and you have to read to be a classical pianist — the way that they went about it made me hate it. . . . I was a disappointment, and at [age] seven it became very clear to me that we had different plans."

The young pianist also took issue with the manner in which composers' works were interpreted. "I remember walking down the hallways of the Peabody conservatory and hearing the same piece being played in ten rooms, pretty much all the same. . . . I knew that I couldn't play this piece better than any of these people. It would probably be very different: you'd know where the redhead was, you'd figure out which practice room I was in. But I'd never win any competitions, ever, because nobody was interested in my take on Debussy. I never won anything. I always got marked down. Always. I had big arguments with these people, that these guys [the composers] were pushing the limits of music at their time, just like John Lennon in his time. To understand their music, you have to understand the time. You have to know what's going on around them, especially when there's no lyric, when it's all music. Nobody, I thought, ever got the feel right. So I knew that if I was just gonna be playing some dead guy's music for the rest of my life, I'd probably never get a hearing, because their impression of what the dead guy should sound like was not mine at all." She felt very strongly that these composers were as underappreciated in their time as rock musicians were in the '60s and '70s. "You get people who embrace [classical music now] but probably wouldn't have at the time. Because at the time, as we all know, looking in retrospect and really studying it, Mozart had a hard time. He was always fighting for his legitimacy as a musician. Some people were in awe, and some people got it, but some were really vicious. Some of these guys really had to deal with that. . . . the content wasn't really understood or appreciated until you could look back fifty years. You'd look back eighty years and finally see what you were dealing with."

As she explained to the *Los Angeles Times*, "I couldn't sit playing somebody else's music for twelve hours and be told that my interpretation was wrong and be okay with it. How do you know how Debussy would feel about my interpretation of his music?" At age 11, Tori and the Peabody parted ways; she has variously described the end of her time at the conservatory as being "kicked out" or having her "scholarship revoked." In 1994, she said to *Spin*: "[M]usically, you can be very broken in certain conservatories and schools and not know your own mind, not develop your own opinions, and you can never be a force if you don't do that. You can be technically proficient but so what? You want to go with me tomorrow, we'll walk down the halls of a conservatory and you'll see loads of the technically proficient — and they're all playing the same damn thing. They've got that Opus XII up and they've got it down, but who's writing Opus XII, know what I mean?"

Patricia Springer, an administrator and teacher at Peabody as well as the organist at Reverend Amos's church, saw that Tori was a "very strong-willed young woman" who didn't fit with the strictly classical education offered. Tori, who would still see Springer from time to time in adulthood, recalled to *All Music* an incident after she left the conservatory: "I'll never forget when I got kicked out of Peabody and I tried to audition again a year and a half later. I auditioned with 'I've Been Cheated' by Linda Ronstadt ["When Will I Be Loved?"]. I think [Patricia Springer] kind of liked my sense of humor, but she said to me, 'You know, what are you doing?' I said, 'Um, I dunno?' She said, 'You don't want to be here. That's obvious. But you've got to find a way to teach yourself a skill, because you're not going to get it here. You've gotten all you can get. You want to be a composer. They're not teaching you how to compose whatever you want to compose. They taught you how to go and do research, so you've got to go teach yourself.' I'm sitting there, going, 'I'm twelve.'"

What Tori was happy to be exposed to during her years at the Peabody were the musical interests of her fellow classmates, which went well beyond the classical repertoire on the course syllabus. She remembers one African-American student, Reggie, in particular: "he was sitting there, playing some Hendrix stuff at the piano. I think he was really into McCoy Tyner also. I would just sit there, because I was kind of in love with him. But I was five-and-a-half, and he was seventeen and black in 1968. . . . [He] had such an influence on my life. I have no idea where Reggie is, but his sense of playing . . . This could be in between classes, but I was drinking it in, going, 'Okay, this guy is onto something here. I've never really heard a mixture of these things. I don't know who this Jimi cat is; I'm five years old.' You've gotta remember, I'm getting it together in my brain. But it had an impact on me."

She learned about Jimi Hendrix and Jim Morrison and John Lennon from her teenaged classmates, as well as from her older brother who brought their records home. As she told *Blender* in 2002, "I loved contemporary pop: The Beatles, Elton and Bernie, Joni Mitchell, Laura Nyro, Stevie Wonder." She would sing to the *Let It Be* album cover, staring at Paul and John ("I kind of had a thing for them because they were the writers and I felt very close to the bards"). Tori's first concert was "Elton John in about 1973. At that time Elton was quite controversial in the States — his drugs, his clothes, being gay. I got there really early with my girlfriend. She was fifteen and I was eleven. We were very mature for our age though; we had a little lump of hash in our back pockets. We snuck ourselves down to the front, we just pushed our way through, and when he threw his water, it fell on me, and I felt like I'd been baptized by the piano king."

Amos had begun composing original instrumental music by age seven, but it was not a deliberate act, as she explained to *Performing Songwriter*. "You're not even aware of it when you're little, what you're up to sometimes. You're just experimenting and you're in your own world. And you're not always analyzing your world that young, unless you're a little Jungian person [laughs]. But I think for the most part you create. Instead of sitting there thinking about what you're going to do and then doing it, you're just doing all the time." It didn't take long for her to start approaching songwriting a little more thoughtfully: "I became much more aware of structure. I think as a little girl I was aware of possibilities, but when I was eight or nine I became more aware of form, and that, yes there were different forms, and what was I going to choose to experiment with."

In her life outside of being a child prodigy and budding songwriter, Tori felt outcast. "I was hated at school when I was nine — a freak child. When I look back at that little girl, she's such a sweet pea; she's not a nerd." As an adult considering her childhood, Tori Amos is able to see how her experience at Peabody and as a musical prodigy shaped the path she took as a performing artist, and she has a respect for the training she received: "I mean, you just know in my style that I've been exposed to things that weren't contemporary music." On the other hand at the Peabody Institute, "people weren't encouraged to think for themselves. That's what we're missing. And not just in music — how to be your own thinker. Give the kids tools, so they can go build their own houses, not the blueprint of what the house should be."

In 1994, as she told *Spin*, during the tour following the release of *Under the Pink*, "The Peabody was at the concert the other night in Baltimore. The dean comes up to me and goes, 'I'm so sorry.' But he also says that I wouldn't have the sense of experimentation that I have now if I hadn't left."

* * *

While the distance of years has provided Tori Amos with a perspective on her time at the Peabody Institute — "I should have been rejected. It wasn't the right thing for me at the time." — it was different for the child who felt she'd failed her parents and teachers, unable to be the classical pianist they once hoped she could be. "I had times then when my spirit was broken," the singer told the *Manchester Evening News* in

1991. "I remember when I was eleven and I thought my life was over." Tori felt that while her mother realized the Peabody was not the right place for her, her father was disappointed. "He's big on education — even at a later age, he wanted me to get my doctorate in music. I said, 'Dad, I don't think people really care when they're buying my records whether it says 'Doctor Tori' or not.'"

Tori's relationship with music and the piano changed in her pre-teen and teen years, following the "failure" at the Peabody. She refocused her energy on her own compositions as well as on the necessary business of growing up. As a junior high school student, outside the world of her musical gift, Tori took the same steps as her peers. A first kiss — "really gross and sloppy" — at age 12 and her first time experimenting with drugs also around this age, as she recalled to Q in 1995: "The first drug I took was pot. I was twelve. I guess that seems young, but this was a different time. We're talking 1974, '75. Led Zeppelin were kicking! It was a different time! When I was twelve, I was smoking weed at a friend's house and my father came to pick me up early. And we'd smoked so much. I'm like reeking. I lied my ass off. I told him my friend and her brother had been doing stuff. But not me. Then we had to go out to dinner with someone from the local church and his son. Halfway through, the son, who was about eighteen, took me to one side and said, 'You are sooo stoned.' Still, I got away with it."

Just like for the rest of the teens attending Eastern Junior High School in Silver Spring, Maryland, in the 1970s, "there was a lot of peer pressure regarding drinking and drugs. But my older sister, who's a doctor, gave me a great gift. She drummed into me that there is a cause and effect with that stuff. I've experimented with a lot of things — I think it's a part of growing up — but I realized if you're going to take that drink, you had better be surrounded by people you trust, because you'll let your guard down." Still, listening to Jimmy Page and smoking pot was not unusual in teen culture in the '60s and '70s. Said Tori, "That was a completely different time, the revolution of many young people against the bourgeois normal."

Amos admired rock legends like Jim Morrison and John Lennon but it was Led Zeppelin that changed her. "I first heard *Led Zeppelin*

II when I was eight or nine," she told *Mojo* in 2001. "I was downstairs in the rec room — television, record-player, shag-pile rug. My friend Linda Yon had lent me the album, and when I put it on my whole body started shaking. Initially, it was Robert's voice. I knew I needed it in my life and quick . . . Up until then, I'd never understood what the men in my father's church were trying to keep me away from. I didn't get why they'd want to shield me from The Beatles or even the Stones, but as a little girl going into adolescence, I knew exactly why they wanted to keep me away from this record." While she was "plotting ways to give Robert Plant [her] virginity," her love for Led Zeppelin also influenced her musically: "I'd been playing piano since I was two-and-a-half, but now I realized the importance of passion. . . . Zeppelin as a whole influenced my sense of melody."

While the rigidity of the Peabody hadn't suited Tori's sense of musicianship, without that instruction she was adrift; her father wanted to find a way to reconnect her to her gift. Said Tori, "I was kind of circling the drain for a year, a year and a half when I was eleven, twelve. I was at the piano every day, doing my own interpretations of things, composing, and [my father] said, 'What do you want to do?' and I said, 'This kind of stuff.'" Her father helped her take the first step of her professional career: the 13-year-old got a job playing piano at bars in Georgetown, Washington, D.C., to customers that Tori would later call "possibly one of the most appreciative audiences I've ever had." Her father was there to support and encourage her, saying, "'You have to start from the very bottom and learn your craft.' He probably imagined someone like Ginger Rogers — a girl who can play and dance and sing and who has a mind of her own [laughs]. But from that point on he supported me totally."

As he explained to *Rolling Stone* in 1994, the Reverend Dr. Amos took Tori to Georgetown clubs, Mr. Henry's and a "mixed clientele" bar called Mr. Smith's Tiffany Room, "when she was thirteen or so . . . and got her a job and then another job playing in the clubs. It wasn't easy taking a teenager to play in a lounge. I often wonder if I hadn't had on my clerical collar, if they would've even talked to me." Tori fondly explained that she owes her father so much for his support and faith in her dedication to music: "It was Dad's idea. These [gay clubs] were the only places that he would let his baby play! And we were a *pair*. Dad in his clerical collar at the back. Me in my sister's polyester pants, all made up, thirteen trying to look sixteen. But at least Dad didn't have to worry about lecherous guys trying to hit on me. Fact was they were more interested in him." It may not have been her father's original plan for his daughter's musical career, but he felt it was his duty to encourage her gift in whatever way possible — sometimes at the expense of his own reputation. As he told *Alternative Press* in 1998, "Do you know any Methodist ministers who would take their daughters to sing in bars? I took a lot of criticism for that. Other clergy thought I was sinning, driving my daughter into dens of iniquity." Tori's mother felt this job performing would refocus her daughter's energy on music as opposed to the culture of drugs and partying that other teenagers were involved in. (Chaperoning Tori provided Mary Ellen with a new experience herself: she'd never been in a bar before.) Though Tori had a complicated relationship with her parents' religion, she was in church choir until age 15 and acted as choir director until age 21. And the congregation came to terms with her out-of-church activities. As Mary Ellen told the *Sunday Times Magazine*, "There was a vote in the church about whether they could support the minister and his wife. We said we had to back our daughter or lose her, and they voted to support us."

Playing in bars gave Tori a much different but just as vital education as she had received at the Peabody. Her audience wanted to hear songs they knew, to sing along; performing other artists' work — "exploring another composer's sonic shape" — made her understand the range of possibility open to a songwriter. "Playing in a bar makes you become very much a one-take person," she told *Piano and Keyboard* in 1993. "The experience teaches you that if you weren't present on that tune, you can't go back and get it, you have to let it go and move on to the next tune. It's very good for putting you in the moment. You're not six songs from now, you're not two songs back, you're in this measure and you're singing this note and you're in this phrase. You have to *live* in this phrase." She described herself as a "human jukebox" (she ballparked the number of songs in her repertoire at 1,500): "The experience was fantastic. I played standards — a little Gershwin and Cole Porter, your Billie Holiday stuff. I'd also do whatever was current — Zeppelin, Carole King, Billy Joel, Elton John. Gloria Gaynor's 'I Will Survive' was a biggie. You had to do 'Send in the Clowns' and 'Feelings' at least five times a night. Plus your Beatles and Stones catalog." In 1991 in an interview with *What's On*, Tori captured the oddity of her formative years: "It was like my apprenticeship but it was also like leading a dual life. Can you imagine, at the age of thirteen playing clubs [on] the weekend after attending school all week?" Her weekly gigs lasted through her teen years and Tori feels she was "kind of brought up, taught how to be a woman in some ways, by the gay men in my life." Explaining to *Between the Lines*, Tori revealed: "They taught me how to put a dress on, be confident, put lipstick on and, most of all, to believe in myself. I was kind of a tomboy. Shy. The only time I was confident was when I was at the piano. By being around the gays, I learned a lot about coming out of my shell. A lot of the ideas and concepts I hold today were given to me at an early age by gay people."

As she grew comfortable in front of a crowd, she observed the clientele as she entertained them: "I was playing two blocks from the White House at fifteen, which really began to shape me as a writer. The congressmen and their lobbyists would come in — yes, with their wives, but also with their rent boys and their call girls." Exposure to the political underbelly informed her understanding of her country's government while providing her with inspiration for her songwriting. "I went from church, which was very patriarchal and authoritarian, to that world, which was very patriarchal and authoritarian. . . . They sat at my piano and told me stuff all the time. I was fifteen, I was sixteen. They didn't think I was going to write about them."

When she wasn't earning her chops playing in clubs, Tori was at Richard Montgomery High School in Rockville, Maryland, and admits that her persona didn't translate off the stage: "[W]hen I stepped out from behind the instrument, I felt like a blushing idiot. I was so confident as a musician, but so unconfident as a girl." She detailed her place in the high school hierarchy to *Rolling Stone* in 1998: "I was kind of a nerd in high school. I never really fit in, but I had a little bit of status because I was playing clubs. And I got along with the minority groups really well. I never liked bullies — I have a lot of time for the nerds of the world, the ones that don't make the cut. I'd hang out with the science kids." Just as she hadn't taken to the rigidity of study at the Peabody, Tori's temperament didn't suit the pursuit of straight As or winning essays. She loved history, cultural studies, art, architecture, and of course music. When she was fifteen, after two years of playing in clubs, she was allowed to go unsupervised and her education there formed a curious counterpoint to her life at Richard Montgomery High: "I found myself working with women who were in their late twenties, and chatting to gay men all night, interrogating them about their sex lives. I got to see a different side of things. Then I'd go to [school] the next morning and it was a totally different experience. I learned to create these different sides to me to deal with it all."

It was also during this time that Tori first began recording music, and she submitted her demos to producers, complete with her father's introductory letter on church stationary. She received rejection after rejection: "They just kept saying the girl and her piano thing was over, [that] Carole King was the last." Tori recorded a song "called 'Walking with You,' and then I did a couple of other things around that period that were separate from that session. They were done in a church. Michael, my brother, was there — he's almost ten years older than I am — and I was about fourteen. Those were called, 'All I Have to Give,' 'More Than Just a Friend,' there was a song called 'Just Ellen' . . . I recorded a lot of things at that time."

Tori's sometime piano instructor and organist at the church, Patricia Springer had faith that Tori would find her place musically: "I always did think she'd be important. I knew that she could make it in the music industry. I just didn't know how . . . She could play Beethoven sonatas wonderfully. One day during practice she asked if she could play her own songs, so I dragged my kids down to listen, kicking and screaming. We were all totally blown away." Tori entered talent contests and auditioned for bit parts whenever a pianist was called for. She beat out a then unknown Sarah Jessica Parker for a part in a Cornflakes commercial: "It makes me giggle to think about it

... They needed a piano player. Could Sarah Jessica Parker play piano? No." Tori's teenage years were certainly unusual but she "wouldn't give up those years for anything," as she told the *Washington Post* in 1992; those years spent playing in bars, making demos, and finding her way as a performer gave her invaluable training for her future career.

It was around this time that she finally dropped the name she hated — Myra Ellen — and became Tori. After unsuccessful attempts to find a name that fit (she was briefly "Sammy Jaye," a name she came up with during her "*Dallas* period"), the singer was given her name by a near stranger: "I was seventeen or eighteen and I was just noodling around [with names] in my head until a friend's boyfriend rescued me. She only dated him for three days but she brought him down to a club where I was playing. I remember telling her I was exhausted going through names. It had been nine months and she knew about the Sammy Jaye debacle. What happened was, he just looked at me. He didn't even know me but he said, 'Your name is Tori.' I went, 'You know, you're right, I am.' She never saw him again. I said, 'Thank you, Linda. You're so selfless. The only reason you dated that beautiful hunk was to get me my name.'" Once the name stuck, her parents took to calling her Tori Ellen, "which is really lovely," says the singer.

Voted homecoming queen at Richard Montgomery High, Tori graduated with confidence, writing a paper in her final year entitled "You Too Can Have a Career in Music," in which she proudly declared, "Nothing can stop me. I know what I can do and I believe in myself." What she wanted to be was a musician; as Tori said to *Seventeen* about this time in her life, "I had dreams, I went and saw them."

Her first stop on her path was a brief one: she enrolled at Montgomery College where she studied music. Tori didn't find what she was looking for there: "I think what you have to be aware of with the field you're going after is 'What are the qualifications you need to do this thing?' For me, what was important wasn't pop stardom, but being a good songwriter. A degree doesn't just give you that title, as you know. . . . I had a lot of musical training. But I just started to feel like the institution [Montgomery College] did not have the right courses to take me to the next step. They could make me a music teacher, a church organist, or a mediocre concert pianist — because there are very few 'great' ones. But they couldn't make me a great songwriter. I had to create those courses myself, separate from that. And that was definitely the best thing I did. Except I should have never gone in the first place."

Nevertheless, she did glean key lessons from her time at college, in particular from one instructor, Dr. James Badolato. "He was a composer and worked for the National Symphony [Orchestra] and I had private lessons with him. I think if you were to ask him today, he probably wouldn't believe that he had influenced me in any way — back then I had this typical 'fuck off' attitude about it! [laughs] But in reality he influenced me a lot, although I was only with him for a semester. We analyzed compositions together . . . He taught me to pay attention to the basic pattern and structure, and not just to rely on spontaneous ideas when composing. Sure, there's something magical when you suddenly feel totally inspired and you think, 'Now is the right time to compose.' But when you just rely on this magic it can happen that you have to wait three years until you feel yourself struck by that flash again. This teacher showed me how I could make something out of one tiny motif, from two measures for example, when I think I have just these two measures and nothing else."

Though Tori's father had wanted her to get her degree, he says of her decision to leave college, "If there's any lesson to be learned out of Tori, it's that her failures have turned out to be marvelous." Eager to pursue her music career right away, Tori decided to move to Los Angeles: "I left home at twenty-one and I was off to the races."

"From child prodigy
to musical joke in twenty years
— how do you reconcile that?"

— TORI AMOS (*ROLLING STONE*, 1998)

CHAPTER 2

Y Kant Tori Read (1988)

Landing in Los Angeles to pursue her career in music at the age of 21, Tori Amos was "just in heaven," not realizing how deeply her departure affected her mother. To the *Sunday Times Magazine*, Mary Ellen admitted, "When Tori left home, it was the worst thing that happened in my life. We'd shared so much. She was always the child-woman. At times it was as if she was the teacher and we were the children. She had this drive within her, and on her twenty-first birthday she said she had to go. We put her on a plane to L.A. and she didn't know anybody there." The L.A. scene in the mid-1980s was one of big hair and decadence, a time that brings out a smile when Tori thinks back on it now, and she adopted a "metal chick" look. "It was a different time; I was in a different place," said Amos in 2002. "Everything was over the top — the high hair, everything. I was shopping at Retail Slut." In an interview with *Time Out* in 1995, Amos mused, "I did what I wanted to do then — it was very adventurous time — don't regret any of it, not even Y Kant Tori Read."

Amos got a job as a lounge singer to pay the rent, singing "Misty" and "Feelings," and the rest of the time she tried to figure out how to break into the business. She'd recorded some demos before leaving Baltimore that could be classified as dance music, but in L.A., the scene was focused on rock and before long Amos found herself as the front-woman of a band. "Y Kant Tori Read was a band that already existed before I came to it," Amos told *Keyboard* in 1992. "They had huge problems, the lineup changed constantly." While Tori was the band's singer, it featured drummer Matt Sorum, who went on to play with Guns N' Roses and The Cult, Brad Cobb on bass, and Steve Caton on guitar. After years of being told that a girl with her piano wasn't going to work commercially, Tori decided to try something different with this band. "I certainly had experienced so many rejections with respect to my music that I began to doubt my music," she told *Visions* in 1992. "I thought, perhaps the people are right, look for a band for you, play dance music, at the moment we are interested in heavy metal and so on. In the beginning I tried to discover new things, and perhaps to learn something, but then I let myself be infected with the virus of the everlasting questions. 'What do you think of that?' When you always had success as a small child, you wonder why today no one is clapping any longer? You become so addicted to the noise of applause that you lose your self-confidence and wonder what you have done wrong. And then you begin to convince yourself that what the people tell you is right."

Said Caton of how he got involved in the Y Kant Tori Read project, "I was a friend of Matt Sorum. We had known each other for a long time. He met Tori and played with her in a piano bar, I think. They started rehearsing and were looking for a guitarist. Matt called me and we ended up founding this club group. I already had some of my own work and Tori helped out by tightening up the choruses. We were in each other's groups for a long time." Of her mainstay group, Amos added, "We were never a metal band. It was just interesting and progressive music. It really could rock. People who got brought into the project didn't think what we were doing was working, although that got us signed."

It was during this time in Tori's life that she was violently sexually assaulted one night after a performance. In an interview with *Mojo* in 1994, Amos said, "[I was] held hostage for hours. And beyond the sexual violation, beyond the rape itself, it was feeling such hatred and believing that I was going to be cut up and never live. When you feel that you're going to be tortured and mutilated. And all the hate this guy has on women, his whole life, is being directed at you . . ." Escaping when her attacker needed another drug fix, Amos found her way home; her mother came out the next day to be with her. "You feel like your boundaries have been crossed to such an extent that there is no law anymore," said Amos in an interview with *Glamour*, "that there is no God. You feel like the mother in you will do anything to protect the child in you from being shredded before your eyes. You're thinking: I gotta get out alive. I gotta get out alive." Amos didn't go to the police, feeling that the perpetrator would never be found and that instead she would be the one put on trial. "With American law as it is and the fact that I'm an entertainer and the kind of performer I was — like Michelle Pfeiffer in *The Fabulous Baker Boys* — I knew I was going to be set up," she explained to *Hot Press*. "And I was not going to be a victim of another experience. But what happened then was that I became a victim of myself." Amos shouldered the blame herself, feeling responsible and shameful, having terrible nightmares, and plagued by embarrassment.

"After it happened," she told the *Los Angeles Times* in 1992, "I buried it. I became *this is over with*. I became *we move on*. And I don't recommend that for anybody." Calling the assault "so totally life-changing, totally incapacitating," the damage done to her in that one night took years for Amos to heal. The hatred she felt "choked me, kept me from my relationship," she said in an interview with *Irish Independent* in 2001. "You do want to punish men. So part of me did become a prostitute. Not in the sense one would normally use the word, but according to the religious definition. I had to be a hooker to have sex. Having felt I let myself and all women down because of my vulnerability the night I was raped I had to tell myself I was in complete control, feel like I was getting paid. Part of me was seething with revenge." It would be years before Amos found an outlet for that rage — and it came in the form of a song, "Me and a Gun," which she wrote after seeing *Thelma &*

Louise and having a moment of catharsis, watching Susan Sarandon's character shoot and kill the would-be rapist. "The big turnaround you make in your head is from victim to survivor," she told *NME* in 1994.

As fate would have it, it was at this time, in her darkest hours, that Tori Amos got what she had come to Los Angeles looking for: a record contract with a major label. "That was a strange time," she told *Record Collector*, "because the New Wave scene was turning into the L.A. rock scene, so it was a really transitional time for making records." Her record company, Atlantic, was looking for the next Pat Benatar, and so hired Benatar's producer for the album, Joe Chiccarelli.

The producer recalled of that project, "It was late eighties, and everybody was in love with the productions of the time, which were much more layered and produced and very involved records — Peter Gabriel's *So*, Kate Bush, Robbie Robertson. So everybody was into making really big, produced records at that time. So we went about it in a fashion to make that kind of record — lots of keyboard over-dubs, lots of processed guitars, and Tori really was after something that had a lot of unusual and big sounds, and wanted a big production. A lot of time was spent back at the little apartment she lived in behind the church in Hollywood, and I would go over there a bunch, and we would sit down and talk about songs, or she'd come to my house and we'd sit and talk about songs, and how she wanted them to sound, and she was very good about describing the kind of emotional landscape she wanted. I've worked with Rickie Lee Jones and Etta James, and they're very, very good at describing the emotion they want the song to conjure up — a mood, a color, a place — and Tori was very good at describing that to all the musicians, and myself."

As a songwriter, Tori Amos felt she had to write what her label wanted out of the band, rather than what she truly wanted to write from a creative standpoint. "I think you would kind of see that that was just me writing with a band in mind," said Amos to *Performing Song-writer*. "Then when the record company got involved, a lot of other people got involved. They felt the material was not accessible, and they were pushing us into another place. And I came up with some songs at the time to try and meet that demand." Chiccarelli recalled, "I never knew it was a band and was never told it was a band until I saw the album review in *Billboard* magazine. While we were recording, it was always a solo project, always Tori Amos, and she had a band that she had done a brief amount of shows with before we started recording, so that was strictly a marketing move because at that time, everything was about bands. And everybody at the record label, including Tori and her management, thought it would be a wiser move for her to be marketed as a band, as opposed to as a solo artist." On the difference between the band that existed and what was captured on the album, guitarist Steve Caton told *Best* in 1999, "The album wasn't even entirely recorded by us. There was a lot of production — some thirty musicians. It was very different from what we had conceived in the clubs."

"*Y Kant Tori Read* was a pivotal point for me as a writer. Some of the things on it work, some of them don't," Tori said simply to *Performing Songwriter* in 1998. Some of the album's tracks were co-written with a musician Chiccarelli hooked Amos up with. As he remembered, "Kim Bullard was a keyboard player I worked with at the time that I brought in to do some programming, and who actually co-wrote with Tori. I got them together early on before we started to work together, have Kim work on arrangements with her. They would send me cassettes of what they were coming up with in pre-production and I would critique it, so Tori spent time with him [before recording] at his house working out ideas for some of the songs. They co-wrote 'Cool on Your Island,' and most of the synths on the record Kim played. All of the acoustic piano Tori played, and some synth parts as well when she got a certain idea in her head, we were all open to 'You know what, you go ahead and play this.'"

Tori was pleased to be working with Chiccarelli because of his previous work, "a lot of groovy records, Oingo Boingo and stuff," and because she learned a number of record-making basics on this first album. As she said to *Record Collector*, she learned "a lot of simple fundamentals that you apply when you're in a producer situation. And that was a gift. Like, never do a take with the band right after they've eaten; don't do punch-ins because the tempo's going to slow down; or, if you're doing a substance, stick with that substance 'til you've done the overdubs!" Chiccarelli, for his part, felt working with Amos was "kind of like working with my sister. She was just a really good comrade, we were buddies, and had a really great time together in the studio. We were silly, and the atmosphere on everybody's part was positive and upbeat. She was great, she was specific, a pleasure, she was passionate, and easy — never demanding — but could be very specific in terms of colors she wanted."

On the drums for that album was Matt Sorum. Said Chiccarelli, "Matt's a fantastic drummer and was a pleasure to work with in the studio. He hit really hard and loud, has great time and great ideas as a player, and that much made the recording easy. Tori had mentioned him to me, and at the time [he] was a new guy getting his start in L.A., and I said, 'Yeah, let's use him on the cuts that are appropriate,' which turned out to be the more rocky kind of cuts that I determined he did best after working with him in the studio for a few days, and those are the cuts he remained on. Those songs that seemed to need more subtlety and a more jazzier feel, if you will, a lighter feel, I brought in Vinnie Colaiuta, who is still a top session drummer in L.A., an old friend and someone I'd worked with a lot and had good communication with in the studio. I thought he'd be appropriate and he was. At the time I also wanted to try different bass players, because again we were really going for this big, layered produced record that Tori wanted at the time. So I brought in Kim Landers for a portion of the album, and Fernando Saunders, who played with Lou Reed, for a portion of the album — so it was really kind of mix and match toward the end of getting the right textures for each song."

Drums were recorded at Sound Castle and Hollywood Sound Recorders; Chiccarelli detailed the technical setup: "When miking the drums, I would have used a Shure 57 on the snare drum, AKG 451s on the overheads, a 421 on the kick drum, and some room mics, a U 47s and 87s. Over the drum kit also, at that time, I was using a Shotgun snare drum mic, which was something they used at sporting events for announcers. I would place that way, way, way above the drummer's head, maybe ten feet high, which gave the snare a little extra crack. I did that on all the drum tracks."

The rest of the band was tracked live off the floor, Chiccarelli recalled, "but did a fair amount of overdubbing. It was a very layered, produced record that Tori wanted — she really wanted a record that had a lot of clever keyboards and arrangement ideas, so things were very labored and layered as well. And it took a very long time to make that album. We worked at several different studios, and it definitely wasn't a bang it out kind of process. We were over at Paul De Villiers' studio, and he had a lot of keyboards there, as well as an acoustic Yamaha piano, which we used on the album. We did some tracks at Capitol Studios on their Steinway, but most of the pianos we used were C7 Yahamas. At the time, my miking would have been a pair of AKG C 12s. It was also the time of MIDI — where you combined two and three synths together to make one sound, so a lot of that sort of thing was done. A Prophet-5 keyboard would have certainly been involved on a lot of things, Kim was a big fan of that; there was also a Jupiter 8 used and a Moog."

Of the album's guitar overdubs, Chiccarelli recalled, "Steve Caton played a small portion of the guitars on the record; a lot of the guitars were done by Gene Black [Steve Farris from Mr. Mister], he did most of the guitars. The guitar rig would have been mostly Marshall Amps, along with some higher-power amps — BHTs and Bogners — those kinds of amps. But mostly Marshalls, fifty and one hundred watt stacks. It would have been the guitar player's choice, but I don't think we did many guitars on that album that were small-amp kind of guitars. They were mostly bigger, layered sounds with a lot of processing, whether via stomp boxes and the Eventide H3000 Harmonizer effects box, which I used a lot on that album."

Once guitar and synthesizer overdubs had been laid down, attention turned to recording lead vocals. Said Chiccarelli, "When Tori was tracking vocals, some songs went very quick, but on others I remember she really took direction well with the vocals, and really wanted to work hard. And with her, it was always about delivering the right emotional performance. An exotic thing we did on the record was with Tori's vocal mic. We were trying out a lot of different vocal mics for Tori, and things like a Telefunken 251 and brighter, airier mics sounded good on her. But we just happened to come across this Swedish mic called a

Milab vip-50, and I think somebody had loaned it to me to check out. But when I tried it on Tori, it really sounded great, so we used that on the majority of the album's vocal tracks.

"I remember ["Fire on the Side"] was really difficult for her — because with her, she really had to put her whole self in the song emotionally, so that one was a tough one because it dealt with a period of her life I don't think she really wanted to re-experience, if you will. So it was a song we did two and three times to try and get it right, even to the point where I had to get her in kind of a charged-up emotional state for her to really deliver the song. And she did, and when she was in the right frame of mind, I think the vocal went down in one take from top to the bottom."

Mixing on *Y Kant Tori Read* wasn't a difficult process as the producer recalled. In terms of the album being remembered as "pop metal," Chiccarelli isn't sure where that genre designation came from. "I never felt that it was a pop metal record, I don't know where the metal comes from other than the cover photo. I remember her boyfriend Eric would come by the studio often, maybe every other day, and he definitely would offer opinions, positive or negative. But he was very supportive and a great guy to have around. Tori knew what she wanted. 'Pirates' might have been her favorite track on the whole album, she loved all the crazy sounds that Kim Bullard came up with, and all the weird textures that were on there.

"My favorite moment in the whole making of the record was, when the album was done and mixed — maybe a week or two later — Tori called me up and said, 'You know, I love my album, this is exactly what I wanted. I really love this album, I'm so proud of it. Thank you so much for making the record I wanted. This is who I am,' so that was one of the most rewarding moments of my career. Whether or not the record was a commercial success or flop — it didn't matter to me. The fact that I was able to help her make the record that she had in her head. That's what a producer's job is, and I'm proud that I was able to achieve what she wanted for her first record."

Still, in spite of how happy artist and producer were with what they'd produced in the studio, once they'd handed the album in,

things took a turn for the worse. Chic-
carelli recalled, "It sort of breaks my
heart because one thing you try to do
with an artist is make the album they
want and follow their direction. And
you don't always agree with it, you fight
for what you believe, but for me, it was
the first time I delivered an album that
was exactly what the artist wanted. And
at the end of the process, she was just
flipped out over the album; everybody
within her circle loved the album. And for it to get so slammed in the
press because of a cover that . . .

"To be frank, I actually brought her to tears — I will never forget
the day, we were in the studio at the Grey Room mixing up in Laurel
Canyon. And they brought in the proof of the album cover from
Atlantic New York, and she showed it to me, and I remember saying to
her, 'Tori, you can't put this out, you can't do this. This looks like some
New Wave tramp on the cover. It doesn't make any sense. This cover
doesn't look anything like the music; it looks like some rock chick
singer. I just don't know what people are going to think, the record is
this layered kind of deep record, and this says slutty rock chick on the
cover.' I remember we took a walk outside while they were mixing, and
I just told her point blank that I just thought this was a bad idea for the
cover, and that she shouldn't do it. I remember bringing her to tears,
and she said, 'No, this is my pirate cover, I love this cover, I love my
sword.' I remember I'd given her that sword as a Christmas gift because
she was always talking about pirates and she had this thing for pirates
and the sword — not thinking it would end up on the cover. But she
loved this cover at the time. So I remember bringing her to tears, and
she was very upset that I didn't like the cover, and I said to her, 'Look,
it's not my choice. You have to go out being represented in whatever
fashion you feel is right for you.' So I actually suggested — based off
this Monty Python cover I knew of, a classical music cover, where the
Monty Python guys had scribbled over it with a black pen — 'Here's

some way to fix it: what if you do like the Monty Python cover, and put a big X over this, or scribble over the girl's face as if to say, "This was a mistake. This is not what's inside."' I remember she went over to her boyfriend Eric Rosse's house, and Eric's mom suggested she withdraw the lettering and draw the creatures that ended up on the album cover. So that's as far as we took the idea of scribbling on the cover, and where it ended up, what the artist came up with was a few of these little white pencil drawing characters around the border of the cover, and so it never was even executed. So the minute everybody saw that cover, they all thought she was a heavy metal vixen, and it really had nothing to do with the music."

In an interview with the *Washington Post* in 1998, Tori reflected on her state of mind then, "I was trying to make myself into something they felt they could package . . . I tried to write songs for the market and some of them still have pieces of me in them, but I was doing it for the wrong reasons at that point." To *Alternative Press*, she elaborated on that point, "I was just chasing the industry . . . You just get so tired of your work being rejected. It was about belonging. It was a time when my individuality wasn't working for me — or so they said — so I cut it out." The record sold just over 7,000 copies upon its release and was treated as a "a musical joke," with *Billboard* calling her a "bimbo." Said Tori in 1998, "They didn't mean to be mean about it. They were actually quite accurate. That's the look I was sporting in those days and I was in better shape — I was pumping then. There was a part of me that really wanted to be a rock chick, and I failed at it." Not placing the blame on anyone but herself, Tori acknowledges this as her career low point and asked Atlantic to not re-issue the album after her later success, a request that the label honored. The resulting rarity of *Y Kant Tori Read* has turned it into a serious collector's item among Amos's hardcore fanbase.

Offering an insider's perspective on the way the album was received by critics, Chiccarelli reasoned, "It was a time when *Billboard* magazine was not giving overly positive reviews, and a lot of time, it's really fluffy; with the trade magazines, reviews could be bought. But at that time, it seemed like *Billboard* was shifting to making really bold statements with their reviews. So I was devastated when I saw that review, because really all they talked about was the cover. And no one wanted to get past it. Some of the reviews of the album were positive, but most focused on this rock chick, which I never got. I always felt that's not what she was, not what the album was. Because it was a pop album, with pop textures — yeah, there's some big guitar moments on the record, but that's not what the album was about." Tori, for her own part, shared with *Visions* in 1992, "I wish that the LP would sound the way the cover looks. The record is just not heavy. It doesn't have a clear statement. I mean, when someone plays thrash metal, then that has a point of view. And even if this thrash consists of nothing but noise — that has a point of view. That should be the point of every publication. Take a clear position, if you want to make noise, do it; if you only want to be cute, that's also okay. But at the time the album was created, I was not able to take a clear position. . . . I believe that the record has its moments, but I tried too much to be everybody's girl, because I was not able to listen to myself."

When the album flopped, Tori was in a bad state, feeling humiliated and lacking self-respect and self-confidence. To *The Face* in 1994, she described one day going into Hugo's, a restaurant where she was a regular: "There were two tables of acquaintances of mine in the industry and they ignored me . . . It's not like I'd call them friends, but I thought they were good acquaintances. One was a publisher — and you know he would give one of his balls to have my publishing now — and the other was an A&R person. One of them turned away and pretended I wasn't there. And the other one turned away and was sniggering with his girlfriend. And she was laughing at me." Said Amos to *Rolling Stone*, "I understood for the first time that I was a joke. And I walked out of that room going, 'They can laugh at me, but I'm walking out of this place with dignity. Hair spray and all.'"

But Amos's self-confidence was shot. And her parents, justifiably, were concerned for her. Her mother said to the *Roanake Times*, "It is such a devastating event when your whole life is in this one product and it fails . . . She really went through a long period of depression. We wondered if she would ever come out of it. As parents, we really wondered if she would ever play again." Not long after the album's release, her band broke up. It left Tori with no choice but to change direction. She now considers *Y Kant Tori Read*'s flop a gift, a bomb that shocked her back into being herself and following her instincts. As her father said to *Alternative Press*, "What it did for Tori was send her back to her piano."

Returning to the instrument she first fell in love with changed the course of Tori's life. "Some people lose their way in the middle of their career," Amos told *Q* in 2004, "I lost mine early on. That's the way you want to do it."

"Everyone told me this
me-and-my-piano thing
was never going to work."

— TORI AMOS (*NEWSWEEK*, 1996)

CHAPTER 3

Little Earthquakes (1992)

"I could not have written *Little Earthquakes* without skinning my knees . . . at a certain point you go, 'Well, what is my thing? Who am I? What am I all about?'" Those were the questions Tori Amos had to ask herself before she could release a second album for Atlantic. After the sting of failure with *Y Kant Tori Read*, she retreated from music. It was a friend of hers, Cindy Marble, then singer of a band called The Rugburns, who helped her find her sound. Cindy asked Tori to play piano for her — and Tori played and played for hours. Tori recalls the advice Cindy gave her: "You play your piano and you sing your songs. That's what you do. And you've been trying to get away from it and be Lita Ford or somebody for the past five years, but *this is what you do*. Doesn't matter if it's hip or cool or not." Despite the fear of failing again — and this time truly exposing her artistic self — Tori decided that she would take down the walls, be herself, and write music that was true to her own vision, and not in imitation of anyone else's style.

The process of writing songs began with literally reintroducing her instrument into her home. "I didn't even have a piano in the house," she told the *Los Angeles Times* in 1994. "I'd trashed that before. So I

rented this old upright and just started to write what I was feeling."
The songs that would eventually become *Little Earthquakes* were not
originally conceived as material for her next album. "I was just writing
so that I didn't go crazy. I wrote for me. I wasn't thinking about making
a record: I knew that one had to come eventually, that's how things
work if you're not dropped by your label. They do expect another one
before you die . . . But, you see, I was working on the dying part, so
making another record wasn't first and foremost on my mind." With
her realization that she "had to do music for the mere expression of it,"
Tori learned "to not be afraid of exposing myself. And if people wanted
to piss all over it, then I'd just let it drip off the tape." After a lifetime of
trying to please others, Tori had finally decided to put her own artistic
vision at the forefront.

The songs that formed *Little Earthquakes* acted as a sort of diary
of feeling and experience that Tori was finally giving expression to. "It
was like I was birthing myself. It was as if I was in a tunnel and I didn't
know the end. It was the first time I really allowed myself to feel things,
to really feel them as I was feeling them. Not cutting them off, not
trying to censor them. Not trying to dilute anything, make excuses."
Her mandate was not to compromise lyrically or musically in the composition of these songs. As she put it to *Performing Songwriter* in 1994,
Tori felt strongly about the role of the songwriter: "Our job is to get in
touch with ourselves. If we're not in touch with ourselves, how can we
possibly give something to the people out there?" The songs were centered on the piano and vocal — and that meant many hours spent at her
instrument crafting these songs. Said Tori, "[A] good song speaks first
to your soul, your heart, and when your heart isn't in the composing
and you only work with your brain, then what comes out of it is dead
and cold. To compose from the heart you have to give it the chance to
open up and react. When you do that, then the piano answers back.
That's a dialogue you can't force. . . . When you don't have the patience
to explore it, then it's the most boring instrument in the world, but
if you spend a lot of time with it, you'll always be discovering something new." Songwriting is a process of exploration, of creating and re-
creating, fueled by a willingness to let go what isn't working. Explains

Tori, "I'll go, 'I'm going to write four different bridges for this song and we'll see who wins the prize.' And then it's like, 'What if I change this chorus? What if I just cut it in half?' That all happens sometimes. You can't be afraid — and I used to be — of experimenting."

Like for any other artist, Tori's training shaped her; the music and styles she had been exposed to found their way into her songwriting as she drew from a

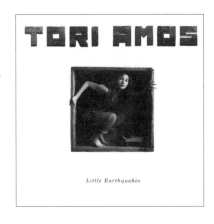

Little Earthquakes

different "chord vocabulary" as someone who favored Bartók over, say, jazz composers. More important to her process than her influences was her ability to detect what was working and what wasn't, as she explained to *Keyboard* in 1992. "[I]t goes back to that belly thermometer. If you learn to accept the first thing that comes to you, then you can't be objective. I listen to a lot of music and I read a lot of books and I know something great when I hear it. It just has a level of greatness and you know it. I can argue almost any time why it is and isn't. But I can't tell you why it works. All I can do is just throw my hands up in the air." Scraps of lyrics could be found on any spare piece of paper in reach of Tori — envelopes, magazines, bills — hastily jotted down before the thought was lost; music and melodies, on the other hand, were always composed at the piano, then recorded with her "boombox" that sat beside her. Providing a metaphor for her process from thought to song, Tori explained, "It's like I have this hunk of clay in my stomach that I'm conceiving. And it's telling me what it wants to be. But I have to put it into a language. I hear it in my head and in my stomach, but the key is translating it into feelings and words." For Tori, lyrics and melodies cannot be forced together, conceived separately, but must be formed together and naturally fit in order for a song to have a soul. Said Tori, "There has already been much too much music that doesn't express anything at all and is only good for dulling your senses like a bad drug. Music should do the opposite; it should open your senses. When you compose you're dependent on these channels being open,

and you have to learn to keep them open and let the energy that's flowing through and filter it into something that's your own." With no overt "message" she wanted to communicate through the album, Tori's lyrics drew on her own experiences and she attempted to channel the musical energy she felt into the form of songs. Her one rule was "no censorship": she wasn't going to play to the presumption that a girl at a piano would be "nice," rather she'd subvert that idea by being raw and open and powerful.

While writing *Little Earthquakes*, Tori drew inspiration from a number of sources: "From Rimbaud to e.e. cummings and from Pablo Neruda, one of my favorites, to Byron and Shelley, who I just recently discovered. Talking about influences: D.H. Lawrence has been a tremendous influence. Right now I am reading Charlotte Brontë. By not reading the great writers you cut yourself from a lot of visionary ideas. And then there are Dylan and Lou Reed, Joni Mitchell and Laura Nyro, all visionary poets in my eyes. Kate Bush is one, too, and the same for Sinéad O'Connor. There are so many, all in their own way. You have to keep fueling yourself. I will never get enough of that. Therefore I don't mind being compared to them at all. It's only human to make comparisons, I do it myself. I see it as a huge compliment because I appreciate the work of those people a lot."

Eric Rosse, Tori's then-boyfriend who she met during the Y Kant Tori Read days, was one of the producers on *Little Earthquakes* and in his dual role was often one of the first people to hear Tori's compositions — sometimes when a song was barely formed. Tori related to *Keyboard* in 1992, "'Mother' was written at six-thirty, seven in the morning. [Eric and I] were on a futon in the little place I had at the time in Hollywood, and I got up really early and started meandering on the piano. I meandered for about two minutes and I started to get [the intro to the song] . . . and I hear this voice from the futon, 'What's that!' And I said, 'Oh, it's shit. Forget about it.' And he yells, 'Play it again!' What happens with each one is that there will be a word that comes with the melody. Then a bridge section will start to work and I'll know it wants to be there. And then maybe I can't figure anything else out, so I'll put it aside. Three months later, I'm walking down the street and I'll come up with four notes, and that's what I'm going to build the next section on."

"Silent All These Years" was very much a song that emerged from Tori's personal struggle with finding her voice — "you can have a big mouth and not be saying anything. I didn't know how to say 'fuck you' to the people who knew every answer about how I should live my life" — and she enjoyed toying with the tension between the lyric and music. "[It] has a certain storyline going on musically that's really the antithesis of what's going on verbally. It's counterpoint, pure and simple. But instead of French horns and cellos or something, it's words and music. And I find it very exciting when an acoustic instrument has its knife out. It can take on these different roles."

The album's most raw and emotionally brutal track for Amos to construct was "Me and a Gun," which dealt with rape, an experience she hadn't been able to talk about but felt it was "freeing" to sing about. Explained Tori, "I wanted to write something so that you could taste it, you are in the car, you smelled and tasted that violation and that fear and that feeling." After seeing the 1991 film *Thelma & Louise*, Tori confronted the violence she'd experienced five years earlier. "[A]s I was writing the song other voices rose," she related in an interview with the Irish publication *Hot Press*, "other voices that had opinions on what had happened. It was then I realized that the biggest mistake I made was not seeking help from people who understood. . . . I finally wrote a song about it instead and *that* has given me the freedom. 'Me and a Gun' is *not* about him. It's more about me forgiving myself. That's why my music now is so therapeutic, so cathartic for me. I made a commitment not to be a victim again, by writing and by singing as often as I can 'Me and a Gun.'" The song was composed a cappella, and she retained that exposed, raw approach for the final track. Wanting this song to be heard by those who have been abused as well as abusers themselves, Tori was still overwhelmed by the response she got to the song after the album's release: "When I wrote it, I didn't know how many women would respond . . . One out of every four women who get backstage say that they have had a similar experience, and that they haven't spoken about it." In 1994, Amos helped found RAINN (Rape, Abuse & Incest National

Network) and served as its spokesperson, taking her commitment to prevention of assault and seeing justice served beyond the power of her songs, a direct contribution she feels proud of. "I'd be quite happy, as an artist, if I knew that a verse, even a line in one of my songs could do for people what *Thelma & Louise* did for me, liberate them in some way, particularly from a fear of the darker side of their own nature. . . ."

Speaking more broadly about the collection of songs as a whole, Tori revealed, "When I go to the piano, another world happens . . . *Little Earthquakes* is that world. I go to these worlds; they're inner reflections of the outer world that I can't figure out."

Recording the album began with producer Davitt Sigerson, but these performances were later scrapped and re-recorded. Tori's label wasn't pleased; as Eric Rosse put it, "They came back [after hearing the tracks] and said, 'What's this?' to this beautiful work." Atlantic Records found they had an artist on their hands who was unlike any other; they didn't know what to do with the piano and vocal–based music that Tori had presented to them. Doug Morris, then CEO of Atlantic Recording Group, conceded in hindsight that he "basically gave her a hard time. When she brought me *Little Earthquakes*, I didn't get into it on the first listen. It was very quiet, very introspective, and for the life of me I had no idea how we could possibly break this artist. I was actually kind of annoyed, because it had been a very expensive album to make . . . It's been my experience that when you encounter a unique artist, it can take a while to get it." From Amos's perspective, "I kept turning in these songs. They'd hear 'Leather' and go, 'You're out of your mind. We're not interested in this.' I said, well, this is what I'm doing." Tori stuck to her vision for the album, and as she re-recorded tracks with Eric Rosse, their budget was tight. As he said, "It was the buck-and-a-half phase where money was really, really limited . . . Everything was pretty much done by the skin of our teeth."

They decided to record the piano and vocals first, and consequently build everything else around it. Explains Rosse, "Pre-production for *Little Earthquakes* was more of a process of sitting down at the piano and making sure the structures were there, and trying to get an understanding of what was going to happen dynamically in each section of the song. And because we were under such constraints, we couldn't just go in and track with a band, and sort of hope it worked out, then re-track if it didn't. So I did end up laying down guide structures with programmed production, where we could go in and nail piano tracks quickly so we didn't burn up studio time, and take it back to my little studio and sort of continue layering.

"We did those songs so on the cheap and I had a little studio in a little guest house out in L.A. I had this old 3M twenty-four-track analog tape machine, a tiny little modified, very compact console made by Allen and Heath, and it was just what we had to work with at the time. And a Yamaha CP80 piano which we miked with a combination of a modified 414, which is not the mic I would use today, but again back then, it was the only mic I had. And I think a couple of times we rented a Telefunken 251.

"We only had a budget of six thousand dollars, so we had tremendous limitations we had to work within, which I think is part of what drove the creative process, and drove some of the inventiveness of the recording process. It was a labor of love, and a love of labor to do that. Especially at the time, it was all analog recording, and samplers were still pretty basic, so if you were working a really tight budget, it wasn't as easy to do things as it is now. We had literally no money to do these extra tracks; it was really hysterical because we were recording guitar amps in a closet. Obviously we went to a live studio to record piano, over a couple of days, using a really nice little Yamaha piano we'd found. What we liked about it was that it was a good-sounding Yahama in a cheap studio. I used C 12 mics on the piano, and I had a couple of keyboards we also used on the record. Right from the beginning I had this great Oberheim OB-8 synthesizer, which I still have, and still use quite frequently. It has great synth patch textural sounds, and then we used other sounds that I created and had sampled, then made keyboards out of."

Rosse explained that during the tracking process, Tori "sang and played piano at the same time on one song ["China"], but for the others, I did not have her sing and record at the same time. Part of that was also technical limitations of what we had to deal with, because for some of the songs, I would lay out a programmed map of the song that she would play piano to. Then we'd go back to my place and really focus on the vocals separately." In terms of the vibe while recording, Rosse explained that "Tori prefers things low-key and relaxed in the studio. . . . When Tori was tracking vocals, she liked it to be just she and I, and at that time, nobody really knew who she was anyway. There was no media, and there were no groupies to speak of anyway. She liked using a little bit of subtle, fairly short reverb with enough to give her something to sing to, and that's pretty standard for me across the board when I work with someone. There are very few singers who don't like anything and just want it absolutely dry, but there are very few who also want lots. Tori's bigger reverbs were added after the fact during mixing. For the most part, the vocal process was very quick, because she's a really great singer. But then, no matter how good the singer is, there are those specific songs that, for whatever reason, take longer to get. And most of the time, it's the singer trying to figure out, and the producer trying to get to, what needs to be the core expression of that song by the singer. So sometimes it just takes a little bit longer.

"With Tori, I recorded everything, even warm-ups, because with analog, you record everything and then make a judgment call, and then erase it and record over it. 'Girl' took a number of takes to kind of get at exactly what she was doing, and some of the others were a couple of takes and that's it." For "Me and a Gun," Tori recorded the song in a single take, saying she had to go into a trancelike state to sing it, which left her exhausted.

When composing songs, Tori considered the arrangement, so she has a near-to-complete idea of what the song will sound like before recording begins. In addition to sampled string orchestration on the album, Eric Rosse revealed, "Some of those [sounds] that you may think are keyboard sounds were guitar textures, [which] were played by her guitarist at the time, Steve Caton. So some of those sounds were guitar sounds we tweaked and [made the songs] quite texturally layered. But for the sounds I sampled, it ranged from plastic hose whirls to different kinds of percussion on cardboard boxes that I tuned down so they'd sound larger and deeper and lower and weirder. Just all kinds of crazy stuff. At the time I used the best mic I had, which was a 414, and because that's all I had, that's what I used. For the synthesizers, if there was a part that was piano-like, [Tori] would play it, and then the textured sounds and programming things like that I did."

Getting into the equipment used on *Little Earthquakes*, Rosse detailed, "Between my little 414 and a combination with a 57 is pretty much what we ended up using to mic the guitar cabinets. As far as cabinets, we had an old Fender Princeton, and we were just coming out of the '80s at that point, so I think we had a Fender Twin, a Marshall Combo, and all of these ended up, for Tori's project, being tweaked and effected and texturized through an EQ and a Pedal Board." Caton himself didn't use anything out of the ordinary to achieve the sound he was after on this record; common effects like distortion, compression, pitch shifting, and delay were in the guitarist's toolbox and created textures that many listeners attribute to strings or keyboard.

In terms of Rosse's relationship with Tori in the studio, he felt that "being musically knowledgeable was absolutely important in the course of communicating with Tori about what she wanted to do on the songs. And that was part of my background, so that was definitely part of what made Tori and I click as a team — our ability to communicate on a musical level. It was also the crazy forces of fate [that] have something to do with it always.

"Where arrangement was concerned, Tori would come in and out of the studio during this process, but for the most part, she mostly left us to it, and there was a pretty implicit trust going on. There was a lot of improvisation that went into the process. So for instance, if I heard that there needed to be guitars or sort of textural guitars in certain spots, we'd look at a particular section of a song and say, 'Okay this needs to be filled, how about something more textural?' Then Steve would get his sound out, start getting his interpretation of what that needed to be, then I'd go to an EQ and tweak it, perhaps take the sound, if it was too bright, and roll out a bunch of high end, run it through a filter, and maybe put an extra little bit of delay on it. Then alter one side of the delay, something odd like that, and create a sound that was not totally characteristic of standard guitar through an amp." Still, there were certain arrangements on the album that Tori was responsible for; "Girl," for example, featured Rosse playing the Kurzweil synthesizer and doing the programming following the singer's arrangement.

For the drums heard on *Little Earthquakes*, Rosse explains, "We used programmed drums on 'Girl,' and 'Precious Things' was a combination of programmed and live, and for 'Tear in Your Hand' and 'Little Earthquakes,' we tracked live drums. For the programmed drums, I used mostly samples that I'd made on an Emulator 2, and I also had a Roland drum module. I also had an old Oberheim drum machine, which, even at the time, was beginning to be vintage. Most of the drum samples were ones I'd actually made with percussion instruments, or odd sounds, for drums. For the live drums, it was a fairly standard drum setup, where we used Neumann 87 mics for overheads and room mics. We'd recorded those drums at a studio called Track Records, located in North Hollywood."

With rough mixes for each song indicating the direction it would go in, Paul McKenna came in to do the actual mixing for the album. Amos was so connected with her music, that in the final stages of creating the album, her reaction to something not quite sounding right was physical. Explained the artist to *Keyboard*, "I know when it's not happening because I have pains in my stomach when it's not. I guess I'm real lucky for that. When a mix is up and I have to run to the toilet, there need to be no words said. You can't just walk out of the studio because you're ill. And I think that when you have so much love for it, it just affects you like that." At the same time, she realizes that she'll never be entirely satisfied. "It always comes down to 'Could the hi-hat have been this, or whatever?' There's always a hundred thousand choices. 'Did I want this effect on my voice?' I go through those things. But hey, they are what they are. This record is what it is. You've gotta stop somewhere. You've got to cut the string."

Once that string was cut, Rosse was pleased with the finished product. "From *Little Earthquakes*, I like different things about each different song, but probably 'Girl' would rank up there as one I'm most proud of in terms of the overall effect of how it came off, based on how I originally envisioned the song coming out. I think it probably hit the mark in terms of how I envisioned it would be and then what it became, and 'Precious Things' was a fun, more aggressive sort of experiment with breath percussion, and different things I hadn't necessarily heard done in pop music before."

Atlantic's initial feeling that the record wasn't working was remedied by the addition of "Little Earthquakes," "Girl," "Precious Things," and "Tear in My Hand." Explains Rosse, "For some reason, Atlantic felt [those songs] rounded out the album, commercially speaking. They were still piano based, but probably a little more aggressive than some of the other tracks on the album. We cut some B-sides as well."

Atlantic's Doug Morris recalled how he finally "got" what Tori was doing with *Little Earthquakes* to *Creem* in 1994: "After listening a lot, I finally got it, thank God. 'Winter' hooked me first, and the more I listened to it, the more I fell in love with it . . . But while I'm slowly falling in love with it, she's sitting in her apartment in L.A. — where all the furniture was made of this soft plastic that would take the form of your body when you sat on it — thinking that I don't like the record at all. . . . So I called her up and said, 'I don't know how to tell you this, but I've fallen in love with your record.' She went, 'Whaaat?' I told her that I had also come up with an idea of how to handle it, and would she like to move to London." Said Tori of her label coming to terms with who she was as an artist: "Half of the staff hoped I'd be a white Neneh Cherry, the other half wanted to make me into a female Elton John. It took a long time before they wanted to accept who I was, and realize I could make them money that way." Amos jumped at the idea of moving to the U.K. "I needed a change. Even though I'd written the record, I was emotionally drained after living in Los Angeles for so long. I needed a new perspective on things, new sights, new sounds. And I needed to get that thing in your belly that says, 'I want to play now.'" She established herself in London's vibrant live music scene. In addition to trying out songs from her new LP on audiences, she incorporated a wide array of cover songs into her set, drawing on her years playing in Georgetown bars. Opting mostly for songs originally performed by men, Tori's song selection focused on bringing something new or unexpected to the cover. "I thought I'd better do covers of songs

that people wouldn't think a girl piano player would do. I do Led Zeppelin's 'Thank You' and I'm working on my Jimi Hendrix. I do 'Angie'
by the Stones. . . . If you give it a different perspective, maybe you can
make something exciting of it." Some of these covers (like "Angie" and
Nirvana's "Smells Like Teen Spirit") would end up as B-sides to singles
from *Little Earthquakes.*

Her label's strategy was to build buzz in England where key taste-
makers could break an artist nationwide. Reasoned Morris to the
Washington Post, "Since Tori could really captivate people, she could
work in small clubs, people would create a buzz and she would have a
better chance of being accepted." Tori agreed with her label's strategy
and saw it working. As did Eric Rosse: "The plan was to release her in
the U.K., build the groundswell there, then bring her back to the U.S.,
which I think was actually a smart move on their part." An EP of "Me
and a Gun" and three other tracks was released in England in 1991,
where Tori finished up the recording of the album, and received positive reactions from critics and fans.

Tori saw the songs on *Little Earthquakes* as collectively dealing with
the "repression of expression, all those thoughts and feelings which
remain unspoken," and found charm in her album's "inconsistency";
each of the songs has its own personality. *Little Earthquakes* gave voice
to the artist who had been unable to reveal herself in the Y Kant Tori
Read days. Said Amos in 1992 of the album, "I didn't write one note or
one word to please people, I didn't do something to have a hit record.
I'm not seduced by the idea of a hit record. If it happens, it happens
in its own time. I'm into making records that know who they are and
make really clear choices." Tori's father felt the album was "about the
structure of a culture that has encrusted your soul to where you are not
who you should be. . . . There's no ephemeral writing from Tori; it's all
out of experience or meaning. As a philosopher and theologian, I think
there's a lot of great wisdom about life in her songs." Released in the
winter of 1992 (January in the U.K., February in the U.S.), *Little Earthquakes* made Tori a critical darling, with *Rolling Stone*'s four-star review
of the album declaring that "newcomer Tori Amos's songs are smart,
melodic, and dramatic . . . That artful paradox is part of what makes

Little Earthquakes a gripping debut." Though the album hadn't been written from an approval-seeking place, Tori Amos received praise and respect for the honesty and artistry *Little Earthquakes* delivered.

But she knew that she couldn't simply try to write *Little Earthquakes* 2 for her next record. "I have to do the next record completely for my own excitement," said Amos in 1992. "I have to challenge myself and get off on the challenge. . . . I can't write 'Silent' again; I'm not silent anymore. I can't write 'Me and a Gun'; my God — I've written that. This record was me coming from a completely unconscious place. You have watched me open the first door — well, that's always the most exciting. That's like the first six months with your love. It will never be the same. Never . . . So I'm a little afraid, and I just have to accept that I won't be your new love anymore." Tori made sure to enjoy the attention and her moment as music's new darling, knowing how "it feels to sit on the tip of a label's kicking boot." With *Little Earthquakes*, Tori came "full circle to just me and a piano. When I ditched it, I had to do it — it was like leaving home. But now that I'm back doing it the way I want to, I can really spin a few heads."

"It sounds naive but the whole time I was writing and recording *Little Earth-quakes*, it never dawned on me that the album might hit a raw nerve with people. I was focused on trying to express myself honestly and make the best record I could. It wasn't like there was anybody waiting for it, because nobody really knew who I was or what I did. In many ways, *Under the Pink* was a harder, more rewarding record to make because it felt like all eyes were on me and I had to really push myself."

— TORI AMOS (*DIVA*, 2005)

CHAPTER 4

Under the Pink
(1994)

As Tori Amos began work on her follow-up album, she made "a conscious choice not to write another diary like *Little Earthquakes*. I'd revealed so much, I truly believed anything I revealed in that manner so soon after *Little Earthquakes* wouldn't be enough, and I couldn't put myself under the microscope again so soon." As she explained in 1994, "I knew I had to change direction because it was like, 'Yeah, we've already seen you naked; now what do you have? Skinless?' So with *Under the Pink*, I put some clothes on." If *Little Earthquakes* was a diary, then *Under the Pink* would be an "impressionistic painting" inspired by Dali and e.e. cummings.

Speaking to *Keyboard* after the album's release, Tori revealed, "I had this whole thing going where I liked codes and going with your senses. It was a bit of a maze, and you as a listener had to work to find out where we were going. *Little Earthquakes* was a bit more voyeuristic. You could sit back and watch this girl go through this stuff. You can't on *Under the Pink*; you have to go through it to understand it. . . . Sometimes I'll listen to work that I've done, and I'll go, 'I'm not in that place anymore. I couldn't write like that if my life depended on it. But I do understand an element of it that I would like to have in, say, this next piece.' I do like that approach of, like, peeling your skin off. Although the whole concept of *Under the Pink* is about peeling the skin off, that's more of an abstract work."

Thematically part of this record dealt with "the betrayal of women, by women . . . The history of woman has been very lonely, and when you think that we should support each other, understand each other, that makes sense to me." But in her experiences, particularly those following the release of *Little Earthquakes*, Amos found that, like most things, this was more complicated. Said Amos, "I've had this idyllic view of the sisterhood that has been shattered over the past year, that [women] would never betray each other. But I was wrong and that's what I write about in some songs on the new album." Tracks like "Cornflake Girl" and "The Waitress" most outwardly reflect this tension. But Tori certainly didn't focus her target on only one gender. As she said, "On *Little Earthquakes*, I went after the Son, so I decided to go after the Father in this one. Bigger game, so to speak." Tori wanted *Under the Pink* to require a more active participation from the listener as well as to explore a "darker space" than *Little Earthquakes* did. "This is not about voyeurism," she said to *B-Side*. "This is not about looking in. This is about you have to crawl into the painting and take yourself there."

When Tori Amos describes the act of songwriting for *Under the Pink*, it is in spiritual language: "The important thing for me is to try and communicate. These songs come from a place . . . that changes the way I think. So if I am not focused when I am singing or talking about them, then . . . they made a deal with me. It's like you have a responsibility to not misinterpret us. If we're going to come to you, you have to respect us enough. I am like the interpreter . . . And because of my experiences growing up, and my musical vocabulary, it comes out in a different way then it would through someone else. I see everything as coming through a source. I am really open to that place. And when you're open, then it is easier to tap into than when you don't believe in it. I am trying to interpret as clearly as I can different emotions through me."

To *Performing Songwriter*, she explained the importance of listening to instinct over trying to imitate what is trendy or might sell. Said Amos, "I'm pretty ruthless, as far as what stays and what goes in a song. I always listen to my tummy . . . Beyond the logical mind there is the tummy. And I really believe this, because we can overthink everything. Hey, I'm not writing things for some genius that's sitting trying to criticize. I'm writing from the tummy, because that goes beyond what somebody else's concept of cool is. I'm so sick of cool. If this world has one more megameter of cool, we're just gonna explode. So it's about allowing yourself the freedom to express. When you allow yourself the freedom, that's your first step. Then the other step is the craft of it, the skill. Okay, so if I don't have a very big music vocabulary, it's not about big. It's about how you use what you know. I think you can stay on one chord for five minutes and make it incredibly interesting, if you know what you're doing. The more that I open my mind to different possibilities musically and lyrically, then the more places I can go."

As a lyricist, Amos revealed that she's "pretty ruthless with lyrics. I don't let anything slide. The music is more stream of consciousness and it's always done first, with a line here and a line there. Again, a line of lyric will come for a verse, then I have to craft around what does this line mean? What needs to support it? Okay, it's a very interesting line, but how I set it up or how I pay it off is where it really means something or doesn't mean diddly. Then it comes back to what I am trying to say here and it gets tricky because I'm not in that trance anymore. I'm just sitting, me and my chair, me at the piano, going, 'What is this girl trying to tell me?' even though this girl is me. So I'm sitting there by myself and I have to try to go into the inner world. It's all about the inner world, songwriting is. Even if you're talking about the outer world, you have to go into the inner world to see the outer world with any interesting viewpoint."

Continuing, she explained, "Everything is tone to me, like what a word feels like. There's certain words that I love, like 'lemon pie.' How it feels in my mouth . . . If I can't see and smell and taste what's happening, then I'm not doing my job. . . . When I'm listening to the songs, I have to feel like I'm living them with this girl that's singing. That's my director point of view. And yet being the writer of the play and also the actor, sometimes it gets a bit self-involved."

In interviews promoting *Under the Pink*, Tori Amos was forthcoming when discussing the inspiration for songs. The song that would become the one she's arguably still best known for — "Cornflake Girl" — grew out of Tori's experience with a girlfriend and drew from Alice Walker's 1992 novel *Possessing the Secret of Joy*. Said the singer, "'Cornflake Girl' is about betrayal of women by women. 'Never was a Cornflake girl, thought that was a good solution, hanging with the raisin girls.' Cornflake means white bread to me, and the raisin girls are whole wheat. So it's Wonder Bread as opposed to whole-wheat bran, whether that's multi-cultural or just being open." In the song she confronts her "naive" notion that the binaries of good and bad can be aligned with women and men. As she explained to *Hot Press*, "Cornflake girls and raisin girls . . . represent two different ways of thinking: narrow-mindedness and open-mindedness and how narrow-minded women betray the rest of us. That division is even there between women, which is something I've really had to come to terms with. It is often women who say I shouldn't express myself as I do and in that sense, women let each other down, not men." This theme extended across songs: "'Bells for Her' is the ending of a friendship, thinking that . . . this is my best friend forever, that only guys do this to each other. And in 'Cornflake,' you think, no, this is not really happening — you bet your life it is. It's a betrayal of women against women, which I really wanted to go into." In "Bells for Her," Amos writes about the reluctant acceptance she had to reach — not everyone would choose what she wanted them to — and that some things will not be resolved. Another exploration of female relationships comes in "The Waitress" where the singer, as she described it, "utter[s] my anger on a woman with physical violence." Explained Tori, "I thought I was a peacemaker, and this violence has totally taken control of every belief system that I have. It's a very scary thing, especially after you talk about anti-violence . . . It's the victims become the abusers . . . where I become the one who wants to slice this person's head off."

"Past the Mission" explores the "trouble in the churches . . . But there's also a lot of hope in that song." The lyrics also explore the idea of reclaiming lost identities: "'Past the mission I once knew a hot girl.' Where is she? Where did she bury herself? Again, it's trying to find the pieces of myself that I have numbed over the years. And there is life past the mission." Reclamation comes up again in "Pretty Good Year," a song that Tori says refuses to indulge in self-pity but retains a tragic element. The inspiration came from a letter sent to the singer from a young English man named Greg. "It was a picture of — he had drawn himself. It was a pencil drawing. Greg has kind of scrawny hair and glasses, and he's very skinny and he held this great big flower. Greg is twenty-three, lives in the north of England, and his life is over, in his mind. I found this a reoccurrence in every country that I went. In that early twenties age, with so many of the guys — more than the girls, they were a bit more, 'Ah, things are just beginning to happen.' The guys, it was finished. The best parts of their life were done. The tragedy of that for me, just seeing that over and over again, got to me so much that I wrote 'Pretty Good Year.'" It was an unusual approach to song-writing — approaching someone else's story — but Tori relished the experience and was so moved by his letter. As she said to *Creem*, "It's a tragedy because I can't make him love himself. I can't do it. No matter how much I beat it into him, I can't do it for him. Funny how the tables have turned isn't it?"

"Cloud on My Tongue" deals with the "concept of free expression in your life. I have it in my work but not in my life. So when I meet these people who have it, I want to get close to them." Acceptance battles with "feeling inferior, that somebody else has something that you want." In "Baker Baker" Amos explored her relationship with Eric Rosse: "I'm the one who was endlessly unavailable, to Eric, even when having sex. And now the only way I'm getting out of all this is with him. The only way back now having taken so much hatred from one man is to accept so much love from another. But it's a long, slow process." Her personal journey fueled her musical expression in *Under the Pink*, and Tori "look[ed] at how I treated men, and on this record, I think with 'Baker Baker,' to deal with a man that truly loved me, but that I wasn't emotionally available for."

As a very loose sequel of sorts to "Me and a Gun," Tori wrote a song that took a different viewpoint on her own experience: "[W]ith 'Anastasia,' I would be looking kind of down on myself through different parts of my life, going, 'We'll see how brave you are.' And I get such hope from that one." Tori bluntly stated that "The Wrong Band" is "for all my friends who are whores." Amos explained to *Free Music Monthly*, "There was this hooker in D.C. that I knew, and she'd been having a fling with one of the governors . . . She got in too deep and thought her life was threatened, so she fled to Japan where she was protected by one of the hierarchy over there. I never heard from her again. It just all came back to me when the Heidi Fleiss thing hit and I started thinking about what that world is about. People don't think of hookers as people, but I quite like them. I find their story really interesting, and when people start judging, they should just shut up because they have no idea what it's like to be on the other side."

In more general terms, the collection of songs sprung from Tori's decision to "rescue myself from the role of a victim. That I have a choice left. Though I can't change what has happened, I can choose how to react. And I don't want to spend the rest of my life being bitter and locked up."

Amos was firm with her label that she wouldn't be working with a hot-shot producer now that she'd reached a level of success with *Little Earthquakes*. Instead she and Eric Rosse chose to head to New Mexico and record there. Explained Rosse, "Tori wanted, in the name of privacy and creativity and all of that, to be out of and away from L.A., kind of in an isolated environment. So I scouted a location in Taos, New Mexico, and we set up in an old hacienda, and did a location production for about ninety percent of the record." Working out of a non-traditional studio made for an interesting setup, said Rosse. "The house we recorded in had a big, great room that we recorded drums in, and then it had a separate room that was our piano room, and we just ran cables all over the house and shipped equipment out there. It was really cool. For the actual input path, we weren't using any console, we bypassed it, and we were going directly through some really nice mics, pre-amps, and directly to tape. So everything was wired through a path-phase such that it went microphone to pre-amp to EQ if there was one, through to compression — if there was compression used on that particular path — then straight through to tape. So there was no console used. The console was strictly a monitoring console, and that was my old Allen and Heath console. It was a twenty-four-input with an additional eight-input monitor section that I would use to run sampler inputs and stuff like that. Essentially, I built and outfitted the studio personally, so we made one room a control room and ran wires to three other rooms for amp overdubs. So I ran snakes all over the house in bizarre, strange convoluted ways, just however we could work it. We had big blocks of foam blocking off some of the doorways so there wouldn't be leakage, we built a big, blanketed foam-baffling system in between Tori and the harp section of the piano. Most of the performances were recorded live piano and vocals, and part of that was that we had the luxury to create that scenario. Tori definitely preferred recording that way."

Describing her producer, Amos said, "[W]ith Eric there are no limitations. He's amazing about that, there's just no limitation. A lot of times, the producer's vision can get in the way. They're involved, and they're creating with you, but they're also listening to me as a writer and where it needs to go from that point of view . . . Eric really helped support that side of me, so that when I go into those places he helps with the whole arrangement of the track, so that they have that thunder and that passion." At the center of *Under of Pink* was her voice and her piano. "My records wouldn't sound the same without the piano. That's why I play alone. Without the piano, my phrasing, my breath, wouldn't be the same. It's like the tide coming in, that pull of sand and sea. It is a relationship. It's the exact moment where you hold that note for that extra millisecond, and you're pulling back on that vocal, and the sustain's riding it all, and you add something in the left hand, and you're holding that note, and then the piano just knows when to come. It's about doing the tango." In building instrumentation around that signature sound, the question becomes "What arrangements can the piano hold?" says Tori. "And through the whole process, we learned the piano can pretty much take anything. It's just this choice, like in that bridge of 'Past the Mission.' I'm playing a Vox organ around the piano, and Eric had styrofoam being pushed on the bottom end of the strings of the piano to create that strange bassoon sound. So there was a bit of prepared piano experimenting."

Said Rosse about the arrangements on *Under the Pink*, "Mostly all the instrumentation — with the exception of some of the programmed stuff — was built around her piano-vocal performances. And getting some of those piano-vocal performances needed to be completely locked down and in time so that drums made sense and so forth, so we had guide tracks she could play to. In those instances, there was more of a programmed guide track, because some drummers can play to a click, but others can't, so usually I had the basis of what would eventually be the final programmed material. Usually I would have the basis of that down, and she would play to that so that the feel was what it should be. So there was usually some skeletal rhythmic structure, she'd play to that, and we'd build everything around it.

"*Under the Pink* was the first time she hooked up with Bösendorfer, so we had a nine-foot Bösendorfer that was just an amazing piano; I believe she still has it. It was a beautiful piano to record on, and we did the entire album on it. For mics, we used a matched pair of B&K 4011s, and those were the primary mics we used. There was an 87 we used as a room mic for certain effects and things, but primarily it was a two mic setup, and they were facing sort of an odd way, non-standard, not in a crisscrossed pattern. One was set up more toward the high end part of the harp section of the piano, and the other was a little bit down in the mid-range aiming at the lower section, slightly apart. So it was a little different, and we just experimented until it sounded right. Additionally, I had an old Yamaha CP80 electric grand, which if you've ever seen U2 in concert and the Edge plays piano, that's what they have. It looks like a baby grand piano in a black, vinyl road case, and it's essentially a chopped-down piano that comes apart in two pieces. It's completely enclosed and has pick-ups running all along the string sets, so you can plug it directly into an amp and mic it. It's a really cool instrument because you can alter it radically by whatever you put it through, and it has an inherently piano, bellish sound to it, and then you run it through something else and it becomes whatever you want to make it. So we used Marshall half-stack amps as well for that."

Back on guitar for this record was Steve Caton. Said Rosse, "We had a Marshall half-stack that we used for a number of things, and then Steve brought a few of his amps out, which included a couple of Fenders, a Vox amp, and a couple of separate guitar-based pre-amps. Then we miked the stacks with a combination for the most part of 57s and a set of micro-check Gefell microphones that is an East German microphone. It's a really cool mic that has kind of Neumann U 67 sound, and we used those and sometimes an 87, and then some of those in combination to get different tonalities."

Caton explained his approach in the studio to *Virtual Guitar*: "I let the song determine my setup. It changes dramatically from tune to tune. This guitar for that song, this amp for that other song over there, and so on. If you learn to become sensitive to what the song is telling you, it will let you know what is working and what is not. In the end, the song is all I am truly interested in."

Rosse selected "a specific vocal mic on that entire record, which was a really nicely reconditioned Neumann M49" but the mic would be of no use without Tori's voice, something the artist didn't have for weeks while in New Mexico. Explained Tori, "I was spraying Pledge polish in a cupboard and I inhaled it and I got a lung infection, which meant I couldn't speak, or sing, for three weeks. And I really thought my voice was damaged forever and had to do voice lessons on the phone, with this voice teacher to try and get the natural cortisone back on the cords ... I was thinking, 'What if I never sing again?' Then I'd say, 'If I can't sing, what's the point in being alive, is this person worth anything at all?' And there were moments where the only answer to that question was 'No.' Then I'd give in to the self-pity that comes out in the song

'Pretty Good Year,' and in the lyric, 'They say you were something in those formative years.'"

Of course, Tori did regain her voice and was able to address both her artistic concerns as well as the commercial demand for radio-ready songs. "On that record," said Rosse, "given the fact that it was a follow-up to the success of *Little Earthquakes*, we both knew and were aware that we needed to have a couple of radio singles. The combination we were after, and my ultimate vision for that particular project: if we could attain what could be considered a pop hit while retaining all of Tori's inherent piano-vocal qualities and quirkiness. We knew we needed a couple the record company would get excited about, and 'God' was one of them absolutely." The guitar sound for that track was introduced while Tori was out of the studio with her friend and assistant Judy. As guitarist Steve Caton remembers, Rosse "had pulled out one of those tiny nine-volt battery operated Fender amps. You know, the type with only an on/off switch and a volume knob. I like to try everything at least once, so I plugged into it, flipped it on, and ended up using the thing for every part on 'God.' The clean rhythm, the crunchy chords coming out of the bridge. All of it, literally. And quite honestly, the noisy bit was the end product of having nothing else to play. It came out of a moment of frustration. I started pulling at the strings, an idea I had gotten from listening to bands like the Lounge Lizards, and Eric had the good sense to press the record button. After immediately deciding we liked it, I went back and did a second complimentary part. The two of us were having such a great laugh because, although it was completely evident that the part was the right one for the song, it was totally outrageous for us to even begin to believe that anyone else would agree. An element like that being introduced into the song that was going to be the single on the new Tori Amos album. The audacity! Anyway, I played the song on my sunburst Strat and, believe it or not, no effects were used other than a Rat pedal for the overdriven chords and some compression. A bit of reverb might have been added in the mix." Tori was reticent upon first hearing it, a reaction that was echoed by her label when they first heard it. Said Caton, "There was so much fear amongst the management and record company people that radio would not play the song in that 'crazy, left-of-center state' that Eric Rosse was instructed by someone at Atlantic Records to make several different mixes of the tune with varying amounts of the Dreaded Guitar Noise, the last mix being completely devoid of it. The different mixes were all put on a CD and sent to radio so the program directors could choose for themselves which version of 'God' they wanted to air. All the business people thought that the mix sans guitar would be the one. Of course, radio picked the one with the loudest noise guitar. A great moment for me. A vindication of sorts."

Another unusual moment during the recording of *Under the Pink* came with "Bells for Her," which Tori revealed to *Creem*, was "written and recorded exactly as you hear it. The lyrics came in that moment. It was almost like a trance, how that song came. It just came through. I was translating as the feeling came through my body. Spontaneous, no fixes. I had to write the lyrics down after I sang them to see what they were." Earlier that day, Tori had said to Rosse that "something will happen today." But, relates Tori, "all day nothing happened. I was standing in the kitchen, cooking something. I didn't dare to sit behind the piano. Because at such a session you must close out your critical judgment. It just happens to you: the music comes, the words, the chords, the singing notes. There is no time to think, 'Oh God, that wasn't a good chord,' because then you're already on your way to the next one. When you feel something like that coming it is difficult to empty out yourself and to dedicate yourself to the process, before your producer. But if you break that enchantment, that's the most stupid thing you can do. Then I'm out of it for weeks. . . . Then Eric came to the kitchen and said, 'Hey, the day is almost over, when will it come?' So I went and played a little on the piano, and there it was. Eric had pushed the record button just in time; it was on it in one take. That was 'Bells for Her.' Now I must learn to play it again so I can play it live, because I haven't played it since."

It was a lucky catch for the producer. As Rosse tells the story, "We had set up this old piano with a friend of mine who also did the string arrangements on that, this wonderful arranger named Phil Shanel. So we took this old upright piano and detuned it and beat it up and changed a bunch of things on it, and that's the sound of that instrument on 'Bells for Her.' And when she came up with the song, she was just sort of noodling around, and I heard something starting to develop out of that, and quickly ran to the console, and I didn't have time to put up a reel of tape, all I had time to do was stick a DAT tape into a DAT recorder, run a quick mic, and hit record and start fumbling with it as she was warming up to try and get a sound. And just as I'd finished getting it going and the DAT was still running, she started into that song and just ran it down, and that was it, that's what went on the album. I think it was happening so quickly that I had a vocal mic on her and one mic I dropped down into the guts of the upright piano, and they went to left and right tracks in the DAT, so at least I had some kind of vocal-piano separation for later, to be able to mix it. So we had vocal on one side and piano on the other, and that happened right on the spot."

Of "Cornflake Girl," Eric Rosse felt that "that song definitely stuck out as one that had a lot of universal appeal, not to sound like a record company president, but it did. It had a universally appealing quality, while still maintaining a lot of inherent quirkiness and Tori-ness to it. The interesting thing about that song is the drums and percussion are eighty-five percent programmed on that, and that basic track is what we ended up cutting her piano and vocal to. Then we put live drums over the basic rhythm track I'd programmed, but ended up only using the overhead mics of the drums, just to give it a sense of live texture. The mics we used on that song for the live drums were a pair of micro-check SLs." The song's unmistakable opening came from guitarist Steve Caton playing mandolin: "There was no intro to 'Cornflake Girl.' I asked Eric to put a click in front of the song so I could play that part. We were lucky that there was enough tape in front of the song. I doubled the mandolin with acoustic guitar, layering a bunch of octaves and fifths. A very simple but recognizable sound. It worked out pretty well, I think." As for the whistle that accompanies it, it's not Tori. Said the singer, "We found it on an Apple computer."

Tori recruited Nine Inch Nails frontman Trent Reznor to contribute backing vocals to "Past the Mission." Reznor told the *New York Times*, "Her music gives me goose bumps whenever I listen to it. . . . It's very rare for music to affect me that way." Amos, for her part, explained, "I wanted him to sing on it because of his energy. I love Trent's work. 'Past the Mission' wanted him to sing on it . . . I did the piano-vocal first, but they played the track, which gave it that — especially in the verses — that New Orleans kind of church meets Otis Redding . . . [O]bviously, it's nothing like he does in his work, which I found an interesting choice."

For the album's rhythm tracks, Rosse "was fortunate enough to have not one but two Emulator E-3 samplers, and at the time, they were fairly new gizmos that were out, and had a whopping thirty-two megabytes of memory, which was enormous at the time. So that allowed you to sample something that was up to thirty seconds long, and that was a big deal. So I had two of those, and they had eight outputs a piece, so I could actually program loops and drum sounds and create and record in there, then edit them all in the actual hardware of the machine. I didn't have anything external, because Pro Tools at the time was really just coming out in a four-track version, and it wasn't as reliable or nearly as known a format as it's become. So that was still slightly out of our reach as an elite tool, and it was still fifteen-bit, 441, so the converters were not as good as they are today. So to my ears, it was not as good sounding a medium as analog or even some of the good-sounding samplers that had been out and worked out for a while. So I had these Emulators and I would build sounds and make sounds, record them in, loop them, build them and kind of lay them out. And even though the memory was internal to those machines, we had external, big optical discs that we'd put into these big, scudsy drives, and it took ages to load in, like, a twelve megabyte sample. But what it allowed me to do was actually run a lot of stuff via MIDI live, because I had sixteen extra outputs between them in addition to the twenty-four-track machine we were recording on. So that was a substantial extra sort of track count for me, where I could run production and things, and didn't necessarily have to print directly to tape. So we could save tape for more drum tracks or vocal tracks, et cetera. Regarding the live drums, while there was a lot of programmed stuff, we recorded a live kit over it."

Compared with her label's opinion of *Little Earthquakes* as Tori recorded it, the singer found herself in a much better position this time around. She not only had the success of the previous album to use as a bargaining chip, but she was mostly dealing with the U.K. side of her label. Said Tori in 1994, "I think the Brits are better because they just know when to back off. They still want the same thing, which is a record, but they know they're gonna get it sooner if they just shut their mouths." Still under the initial record deal she signed in 1986, Tori was now renegotiating terms before each album with Atlantic/Warner Music Group. As she said in 1996, "It's hard to think that when you're in a democracy that someone could own you for twenty years, but I signed it. I try to teach young artists how to protect themselves. It's so frustrating sometimes. I just want to say, 'Put your weed and your skateboard down for five minutes and read [contracts]!'"

Under the Pink, released in January 1994, debuted at #12 on the U.S. charts and at #1 in the U.K., and produced four charting singles — "God," "Cornflake Girl," "Pretty Good Year," and "Past the Mission." Said Atlantic CEO Doug Morris of the artist who had now proved she could be both commercially viable and critically successful, "A unique artist doesn't make records for radio. She should make records she loves, and that the people who love her will love. It isn't the easiest way to do it, but if you're willing to do it the hard way, it can last forever. If you have an artist with that kind of talent, you let them lead, and they're going to take you to places you've never been before. Tori is someone you have to let fly."

Looking ahead to the next record, Tori Amos wanted to emulate The Beatles in that they were "constantly changing and exploring, and no record was like the last one." Said Tori in 1994, "I've got to be a real clever little beaver this time. I just want to challenge myself. I'd like to be able to look at it and go, 'This blows my socks off.' I think if I could say that, I would be quite satisfied. I don't know if I *can* blow my socks off. That's my worry. I've got some pretty thick, tight socks on. But we'll see . . ." Though she had no intentions of resting on her laurels, Tori Amos also relished the place she now found herself, the result of decades at the piano and years spent finding her musical identity. To

NME she quipped, "Now I've avoided the 'sophomore slump,' I've been on the cover of *Spin*, I've had number-one records, but I've got a career not based on hits, based on a body of work. I haven't compromised, I'm in a position to do things in music I thought about for years, and people still wanna hear it. Wouldn't you be stoked?"

"*Boys for Pele* is probably my most painful record. For that album, I really took a turn. I walked off of a really nice road to a world where I had to sort of uproot a lot of things in my life, and for me, it all ended up happening publicly. So *Pele* is sort of a raw nerve. Sometimes I can't listen to it."

— TORI AMOS (*DUQUENSNE DUKE*, 2003)

CHAPTER 5

Boys for Pele
(1996)

The *Boys for Pele* era was one of personal change for Tori Amos: she and Eric Rosse split up after years together. Speaking to *Spin* in 1996, Tori explained, "Eric and I were inseparable, and the truth is I don't care any less for him. We just agreed that we needed to go and be independent of each other. Sometimes I didn't know what was my thought or what was his, and that's not healthy. We painfully held hands and looked at each other and said we have to go explore, we can't protect each other anymore. I miss him of course; you kind of miss it when one of your arms is gone. I mean, I have a really good left hand and it plays really fast but I do miss my right arm. I seem to be growing another one, though, and I think he needed his back so that he could play his instrument."

The loss of this relationship fueled her songwriting and, as it had been in the past, became a kind of therapeutic process for her. Said Amos, "I had to write [*Boys for Pele*] in order to even walk outside of the house by myself. It has been, for me, the shattering of a fantasy or a dream." It was a difficult period for the singer, cut adrift from her old life but not yet grounded in a new self. "When I was behind the piano

I was okay," she revealed to *Keyboard*, "but when I was away from that instrument I was totally out of my element: I just shriveled up, so that there was no woman, there was only a musician — or nobody." Writing helped fill the void in a way that nothing else could. Said Amos, "As I wrote the songs for *Boys for Pele*, I started valuing myself through my own eyes, instead of valuing me through the eyes of others, like the press or a lover or whatever."

Tori offered in explanation of *Boys for Pele*'s theme: "The record is metaphorical in that there are places within each song where it becomes very clear, I think, what the emotion is that's being claimed. Its all about the intimacies of womanhood . . . Each of the songs became fragments. There's a story — you're given excerpts. When you hear the whole record, the story will either make sense or not." While Tori Amos frequently described the songs on *Pele* as fragmentary, she very much felt they were a united group that would not belong on any of her other albums. "I am not about throwing a bunch of songs together," she said in an interview with the *Baltimore Sun*. "I can't imagine songs from *Pele* being on *Pink* or songs from *Pink* being on *Earthquake* . . . they are very much a different story. Even though I feel like they are a trilogy, they follow a quest. This work is more a novel, *Earthquakes* was more a diary, and *Pink* was more impressionist painting like short stories, thoughts, that didn't relate to each other."

In the course of writing the album, Tori Amos realized that everything she was searching for and had been drawing from external sources was in fact inside herself, and the songs explore the idea of reclaiming passion and compassion by bringing home "the fragmented demons of [her] womanhood." Said Amos, "This is about finding my fire. This is about standing on my own. And there are a lot of people that are at the point in their life where they have to stand on their own and face how scary that is." With *Boys for Pele*, Tori had found "complete creative freedom," an experience she often likened to jumping off a cliff.

Her writing process on this album was not strictly structured — she revealed she liked writing in bathrooms, where the acoustics are good and no one hears you sing; that some ideas just popped into her head as she was on the phone, waiting on hold; while other songs took a bit more work. "A lot of the time, to get an idea, I have to have an experience, which helps me to understand what I need to write. Or I'll get a fragment of an idea, and it'll take a lot of patience to get it out correctly. Because that's what writing and expressing yourself is about. If I wrote like I was on deadline for a show or a story — just to get it done — that would be the wrong reason to write. If you write just to finish it, why are you writing? It's pointless. You have to be willing to let the story or the idea develop over time to make it good."

Of the album's title, Tori Amos explained, "Pele is the volcano goddess and the boys are those who have brought me to my fire with what they have or haven't given me." For this album, Amos once again asked her listeners to inhabit the songs in order to fully understand them: "I think with *Pele* to observe from the outside it is difficult to decipher. If you crawl in and take the journey with her . . . and become part of the record, it's almost like an audience participation record, because I do think you have to allow yourself to be in the work to get it. If you're looking out from the work, the imagery might not make a lot of sense, but if you pick something in each song to shape-shift . . . You have to choose to be a character, I think, in *Pele* to really get it, whoever you choose to be. You don't have to be a human being. You can make any choice, but it is about me finding different pieces of myself, different pieces of this woman."

"That's the journey," said Amos, "whatever it took for the eye to see, what was in the heart. I'm showing you the woman both ways: desperation — the absolute obsession, worship — and then at the other end of just disgust. That's what I felt coming through when I sang them; I let myself go there. But some people don't want to take that ride — it's not for everybody."

In an interview with *B-Side*, Amos delved into the album track by track: "The record starts off with the horses from 'Winter' taking us and

we ride. Going into that program of the beauty queen. She's a beauty queen, and that's not enough because it never is. The idea that beauty is our answer when we are four years old, 'Oh, isn't she pretty . . .' That's the first thing that you hear. So it's going after those programs of the feminine, going after them, going after them. To visit 'Father Lucifer,' to have a moment to dance . . . to go down in the dark. . . . [T]hen we go and meet the 'Widow.' Then we pick up pieces as we go. In 'Mr. Zebra' we pick up Ratatouille Strychnine, who we love because she's our little double agent who can poison people and get us out of trouble when they're hurting us! But she's tired, she's tired of the poisoning. . . . And part of you has to die, and in 'Marianne' it's the whole Mary Magdalene reference, a young girl who I knew that died. There's the whole idea of that part of woman that has been dormant, who's been dead. . . . Then we go on to 'Caught a Lite Sneeze' and she's still vampiring, she needs that boy blood . . . ['Hey Jupiter'] is the point where she knows it's over with this particular relationship, or -ships, and it's not ever gonna be what it was again. It is never going back. That's where the whole record turns on its axis . . . Go further into the place of the South, the place of the hidden, with 'Little Amsterdam,' which is all metaphorical, about wanting to kill people, being angry at people that you feel have done something . . . the whole domination thing, the whole hierarchy, patriarchy."

From this turning point, the singer explains, the album moves "into the dance of 'Talula,' and her desperately trying to dance, desperately trying to figure out the whole idea of loss . . . 'Not the Red Baron' is the moment of compassion for all the men on the record. It's where I could see their planes crashing; I could see that they have a side too. And if their planes would crash I started to gain compassion for their side of it. But I'm still acknowledging the war with 'Agent Orange,' the idea of the war . . . Which leads us into 'Voodoo,' . . . the key for me here is he was going to show me spring. Going to . . . and so much of my life has been about going to. Instead of what is happening now, [it's] what are we going to? Not what are we really giving to each other now. What am I promising him? That whole idea of looking to this, the idea that somebody else carries the voodoo, instead of becoming part of the voodoo and accessing it yourself. That runs through the whole thing . . . And, of course, 'Damage' speaks for itself. The song, being herself damaged, it's trying to teach myself about graciousness, and I have such a hard time with that. . . . Yet the record isn't finished until 'Twinkle'; it just wasn't finished until that song. That level of the flame, feeding the flame, because after all the stars, the fire, I had to go into that place of becoming that, instead of trying to find it again."

Expanding on how "Talula" came to her, Amos told *Vox*: "When I wrote this, my mother was sitting in a chair, and I'd been playing for a few hours. She was fading in and out of sleep. I'd been going through some of my blood, guts, and widow's tunes. And all of a sudden I needed to breathe. I started playing 'Talula,' and it became like a breath, 'cause I needed freedom from all these songs that where showing me my monsters. Talula started to show me how to dance. And my mother began to wake up. The song is really a riddle. Talula just came to me, telling me her name. A lot of the times I'm just trying to interpret what I'm seeing on the other side. A name holds an energy, like anything else. Look at Ruby Tuesday. I think Talula became about rhythm and tone and sensuality. It ain't fucking *Catherine*. There's something in there about West Indian dance. And yet it's a very classic name, too. Talula really just started to represent all women to me — women that let themselves dance, for themselves."

"Hey Jupiter," Amos recalled, was written at her lowest point: "I was at a hotel in Phoenix, and I realized that for once there wasn't a man I could turn to. . . . she knows the way she has looked at relation-ships with men and put them on a pedestal is over. There's a sense of incredible loss because I knew that I would never be able to see the same way again. It's freeing, and [yet] there's a sense of grieving with that." The associations Amos made informed the imagery of *Pele*'s songs; Amos explained the origin of "In the Springtime of His Voodoo," for example: "Jamaica, to me, represents the mysteries. If you go back to that culture, they had belief in the spirit world. Some call it voodoo . . . Voodoo became something different once the Christians came in. Before then, there was an understanding of other worlds we have chosen to disrespect. When I say, 'Do you know what I have done,' I haven't honored that world." In "Blood Roses," one of the first songs written for the album, Tori explored the image of shedding her blood to make music but it never being enough. Playing on a similar theme, Amos raised a Lady Macbeth figure in "Professional Widow" to get "all that nastiness out. The truth is, if there's a part of you, of Polly [Jean Harvey], of Bjork, or of Courtney Love, which is the black widow, then you will relate to the song. If people don't feel that way, they won't resonate with it."

Since Amos had parted creative company with Eric Rosse, she decided to produce this album herself; she also recruited engineers Mark Hawley and Marcel van Limbeek, who had worked on her *Under the Pink* tour. Said Tori, "I asked them to make *Boys for Pele* with me. . . . I needed an independence and to strike out on my own, so I pulled this team out. Mark has had studios since he was an adolescent . . . [and from] what I understand, Mark, when he was four, he was a drummer. He was studying when he was eleven with Cliff Richard's drummer. And he picked up the guitar when he was ten, so he was multifaceted, but then was drawn into wanting to have a mixing desk as his instrument. That's his bloodline. And Marcel is Dutch and was a physicist who left school. He's dealing with facts, figures, theories, equations . . . and madness. Together, there was a real push from them. They argue with me. They take a very fierce stand on the engineering thing: 'You need to be aware of the sound of your records.' But sound is an instrument. There's no room for musicians to be sonically shut out and turn it all over to a producer."

Marcel van Limbeek had started out as a live engineer in Holland in the mid-to-late '80s before moving to the U.K. to continue his work there. Said van Limbeek, "One of my best and earliest friends in England was Mark Hawley, who is now Tori's husband [they married in 1998], and I knew him before they met, basically. We first started doing live sound for Tori when she toured over in England, and she loved that approach, and we got on straight away. We got offered her *Under the Pink* tour, Mark was offered to become the house engineer, and basically Mark was good friends with John Witherspoon, who at the time was Tori's tour manager and now is her manager. So Mark got me involved, and we all started working together. We loved working together because we were both interested in high-quality audio — he was a great front-house engineer, and together we were basically a good team." On that tour, the two had recorded some B-sides from the show, which were well received and helped land them the gig of engineering *Boys for Pele* — a working relationship that has continued for years. Of the different roles the two engineers play when working on a record with Amos, van Limbeek says, "I think, if anything, I contribute with audio engineering, finding the microphone, microphone placement, general mixing [and] engineering, compressing, EQing, finding effects — that's more what I do. Mark, I think, does that also, but is really more like a producer with her, so they'll talk about song structure, how a song will evolve. And I'll gladly give my opinion on that, because we all have a say in everything really, but I think over the years, I've become more the audio person and they together produce more. That doesn't mean they have no say in audio, because if they don't like the microphone, they'll tell me about it straight away."

In an interview with *Sound on Sound*, Mark Hawley explained the benefit he and van Limbeek were able to bring to the recording process because of their background working on live performances: "Live sound and the studio are very different cultures and I think that had a lot to do with the sound we achieved on [*Boys for Pele*] — especially on how dynamic it was. Although we came at it from the live sound angle, both Marcel and I love the studio and it's a really great mixture to have the experience of both sides — a definite advantage."

Of the new working arrangement on *Pele*, Amos said, "[My] relationship [with Eric] was really collaborative in the past. I missed that in some ways. But, in other ways, it was so freeing to just do things I really wanted to do. The record wouldn't have turned out the same." To *Musician*, Amos described what working with Mark Hawley was like: "Mark and I in a room together are very volatile; that's what makes it exciting. Mark knows my pictures: he knows when I say, 'Girl in a bathroom,' that Beauty Queen is the front for Horses. He's trying to translate what a bathroom is. He'll scratch his head, look at Marcel, and come up with another element." Van Limbeek felt the three became a team that worked well together with the artist at the center: "Tori's always had really genius ideas in terms of production and what she wanted for the sonic picture she had in her head . . . to combine her musical ideas with the audio and sound quality. I was just there to make things sound good; I was just an engineer, so it was her picture that we all created. She always had a clear idea of what she wanted . . . she's the guiding light, she's the star, so a lot of pretty awesome ideas will originate with her."

Her sonic vision for *Boys for Pele* was freed of boundaries, multi-layered, and diverse. "There are over seventy-five musicians," revealed Amos, "from the London Symphonia to Caribbean percussionists to gospel choirs to different Louisiana brass bands . . . I just kept pulling it together. Working with all these people . . . it's going from an instinctual place and getting all the musicians to know the sounds and tastes and smells, know the characters. I'm translating for them." While the talent on the album came from various places, Amos had to settle on a primary location to record *Pele*: after considering the South for its "hiddenness" (which she said mirrored her feelings in relationships with men), she chose an Irish church. Amos explained her choice to *B-Side*, "[T]here were many reasons. But it's trying to break free from domination: domination from England, domination from the Church, and the domination they impose on themselves. That's how it's very similar. I went after that. I also went after the idea of claiming my womanhood: I had to do that in the church, because that's where it was really circumcised. Not just the Christian church, but religion in general, honoring the female part of god . . . That's why recording this particular album in those places screamed defiance, since both areas still repress women."

After visiting about 10 to 15 churches to find the most appropriate location, they found a church in Delgany, which worked well acoustically. Having found the place to record, Amos's next step was going back to England to get her harpsichord. "I knew I had to bring it," said Amos. "If I was going back to the bloodline of woman, I had to do it with my instrument — so, I went to the bloodline of a piano which is a harpsichord and a clavichord. And I used both of them on the record. The album felt ready to go in June. So, we went on location to Ireland, where we recorded a lot of the musicians. Then we went to Louisiana to pick up the gospel choir, because I was taking my ley line over. Musicians had come from Africa, musicians had come from Paris, musicians had come to take the ley line back in — musicians from the West Indies we brought in. So, the elements of the South — I went to the Old World and brought them over — I brought them into the New World. That's an underlying current of this record. There are many different layers that come in. There's the metaphorical level of the lyrics, but then there's the music which has got subtext, and the different players, and the arrangements, and what they're saying."

Marcel van Limbeek loved working in the church: "The thing about that place was that the acoustics sounded absolutely stunning; they were fantastic. It was a highly unusual approach because basically we tracked Tori first, so all the drums were overdubs basically. The drums were never recorded at the church; we just tracked Tori at the church with her piano and other instruments. She played harpsichord, and [recorded] her vocals, and we also did some brass recording at that church. When we recorded a big brass section in there that was used on a bunch of tracks — to do that in a church on location and we didn't have a mobile truck . . . We did everything using a small shed off to the side as a control room. So to get all the wiring done, and as quiet as possible, was a huge challenge. The whole record was challenging for me because Mark already had quite a bit of recording experience, and Tori did too, but I certainly didn't. So for me the whole thing was challenging. What we did at the time was, because it was such a big project, and was new to us, we very much kept it safe. What I mean by that is we tried to get the best possible microphones, pre-amps, connections, and make sure the technical side of it was as sweet as possible. We also made sure we had a really clean main power supply, because we weren't recording in a proper studio you see, we were recording on location. So that was a challenge to make that work. Because also there was no sound insulation in the studio so every time a big truck drove past, we had noise."

Another issue in recording was separating the vocal and piano tracks, which in the past had been done by muffling the interference with blankets covering the piano. For this album recording with the harpsichord presented an additional challenge, as Mark Hawley explained. "The harpsichord is about a tenth of the volume of the piano, and we were very concerned about her vocals getting on the harpsichord mics. So to try and keep some separation, we built this ridiculous wooden booth construction, which Tori sat in with the keyboards poking through a slot in the bottom — it was every bit as bizarre as it sounds! We made the inside as dead as possible so it didn't sound too boxy, and it worked surprisingly well." In addition to making sure they had clean, separated tracks, the engineers had to capture Tori's vocals in her trademark manner. Said Hawley, "She's so particular about her vocal sound . . . and being able to hear the realness and the detail of it. And very rarely is there much reverb or anything on the vocal."

Van Limbeek detailed the odd setup that Tori recorded *Boys for Pele* in: "There was a slit in the box [that Tori recorded in] between the keyboard and the piano, so on one side you had the piano, and the harpsichord on the other side. So inside this cabinet, we'd have this Neumann M 49 microphone, and then on the outside there would be the piano and the church, so it was like a vocal booth really. So we had that built and it proved to be a big challenge. For Tori's vocals on *Boys for Pele*, Tori had her own M 49 microphone that she'd used with Eric Rosse for *Under the Pink*, and she'd kept that mic, which is beautiful sounding. But it's an old microphone, and it had the tendency of starting to sound a little harsh if she was singing too close into it, or when Tori was singing too loud into it, it had the tendency of becoming quite harsh. And at the time, that was the best mic we had, a gorgeous sounding mic, but for those songs where she'd be quite loud in the microphone, we'd swap it out for a U 87. That mic could handle her voice much better, and that was the first time we started experimenting with different vocal mics. The upshot is that we learned that whenever she sings quiet and with a warm, soft-sounding voice, it works to have a microphone that sounds a bit harder itself, and the other way around — if Tori sings loud, or has a little bit of a harsher voice for the performance of a particular song, it works well to have a mic that sounds a bit softer."

Van Limbeek was blown away by Tori's more spontaneous, creative moments during recording. In one instance, they had a new microphone that needed checking out and asked Tori to test it. "[We said] 'Tori, we need you to check this mic out, but we can't go straight into record, we need to check the mic first.' But the one thing about Tori is, any time she sits down, you always press record. So she started singing into it, and out of the blue — ['Not the Red Baron'] had never existed before that moment, and there it was. In fact, you can actually hear me talking in the background, because I was next to her, talking to Mark who was in the control room. I was setting the pre-amp level, so you can hear me talking in the background. But she does that at live shows as well, where she suddenly has this inspiration — and then there's a new song." Hawley confirmed that on both "Not the Red Baron" and "Marianne," "the first time she ever played them and the first time we ever heard them was the performance that you hear. The whole recording process was really special for that reason."

The microphone setup that Marcel van Limbeek and Mark Hawley established on *Boys for Pele* would stay with the team all the way through to 2005's *The Beekeeper*. Says van Limbeek, "We'd tried a few different mics here and there, and tried a more lo-fi approach for a couple of songs, but generally our technique stayed the same. Basically, we applied an A-B technique to miking Tori's piano, with two Neumann U 87s with two cardioids, maybe seventy to seventy-five centimeters apart from each other inside the piano, with the lid all the way up looking down towards the bridge, where the strings transferred energy onto the soundboards. But not too close to the hammers, with the low U 87 bent to the left and the high U 87 bent to the right, and typically we used Focusrite Red 1 mic pre-amps for that. So aside from the U 87s in Tori's piano, we added quite a bit of ambient microphones up there as well. Aside from the U 87s inside the piano, looking over the strings, we had, a bit further out, two omni-directional DPA mics. They were called B&K 4003s at the time, and they were a little bit taller than me, so they would basically look over my shoulders, much in the same way if you were to mic up an orchestra. You'd put your main stereo microphones right where the conductor is, looking over his head, that sort of setup. And we would mix them in basically with the U 87s, quieter but basically the sounds from the church we got off those DPAS, we would mix in with the dry piano sound. So we'd mix in a dry single with a bit of reverb, if you know what I mean. That's been our piano sound for years."

Of the album's sound, Tori explained her vision to *Music*: "I wanted your head in the piano in all natural reverbs, and I recorded it in the church, and it was much of an organic kind of thing. I wasn't experimenting with seventy different microphones and different compressions and reverbs and gadgets and R2D2 upside down on my head. I was really interested in working with brass and the harpsichord. I went back to early keyboards before the piano. And so there weren't loads of loops, and there weren't loads of synths happening or anything like that. So that record was very piano-harpsichord oriented." Playing the harpsichord changed her as a musician, expanding and changing her approach to the piano. Said Amos, "It's a difficult instrument, it's quite demanding. It takes so much skill, for me anyway. It's really challenging for me to pull it off, but at the same time, it's thrilling."

Van Limbeek explained that instead of recording everything through a mixing console, as would be the case in a traditional studio, *Boys for Pele* went through "a tiny thirty-two channel TASCAM console for monitoring only, and I think it's still one of the many strengths of the album, because musically it's pure genius, but where audio came in, we wanted to play everything safe. . . . The signal for the recording never actually worked through any desk at all, until we hit the mixdown stage. So we made sure that all the mic lines were as short and as high quality as possible, going from high quality mic into high quality pre-amp into the Sony as quickly as possible."

Once basic tracks had been laid in the church, they changed locations, recalled van Limbeek: "Tori had purchased a house in the south of Ireland, and we basically converted that into a studio at the time, and that's where we then recorded drums and electric guitar for the *Boys for Pele* LP. She still owns that house, but it's not a proper studio, we just converted it for that album; it was a beautiful big house with beautiful big rooms." For the album's drums, van Limbeek explained,

"We were really lucky because we were working with Manu Katché; he's a fantastic drummer who gets this amazing sound, so to be honest, that's half the battle. Anyway, we found that in selecting the best room to record drums in, we just put Manu in each room and chose the one that sounded best. What I did a little bit to avoid too many reflections: we had some acoustic foam we stuck on the wall in random places to get a reflection better that was as random as you like. It was placed to stop comb filtering and too many early reflections, and we were also lucky just by the talent of Manu Katché and how good his drums sounded, and just the fact that we got lucky with the sound of the room in the first place. In terms of mics, we used omni-directional DPA 4003s for overhead miking, and we had 4003s also as stereo room mics at the time, in the same way we had them set up for the piano. It's just a great sounding microphone for drums or piano. It doesn't really add like a Neumann does, but the 4003 picks up and captures the real thing in as high a quality as possible. So we used that, and then on the drums themselves, we had 421s on the toms, and on the kick drum, we used a D 112, so some pretty straightforward stuff."

Once principal tracking wound down after about four months, Tori recalled that the team had really gotten to know each other. "You can imagine that when you and your crew are working and sleeping together, you do get very close, but you also can't get away from each other. You try not to tread on one another's tails, shall we say. It was fascinating for me because I really let my whole musical kind of, shall we say, 'spice,' decide what it wanted to pull forth that day. But if we wanted a Leslie cabinet, that got a little tricky, because we were in this remote little county, and I think we got the only Leslie in Ireland that was available. It was partly broken down. We put it out in this graveyard. That's how the record happened; it was very spontaneous as it developed." Though in some songs on *Boys for Pele* "there is actually a lot going on," Tori wanted the album to not make a glutton of the listener: "It's more like spice: a taste of something. Or if you think of architecture, I wanted nothing to take up space, I didn't want you to feel you were walking into a room and feeling suffocated with sound."

Released in January 1996, *Boys for Pele* debuted at #2 on the Billboard Top 200 Album chart, produced five singles ("Caught a Lite Sneeze," "Talula," "Professional Widow," "Hey Jupiter," and "In the Springtime of His Voodoo"), and dazzled critics. For Amos herself, making the album had been a deeply cathartic experience: "I listened to the disc on the airplane all night and I knew. I knew I had left a part of my life behind. I could begin, now that I have finished this work, to open up to new people in my life. I was living and breathing it all during this record." Knowing the album might make people uncomfortable, she explained, "I'm ready to jump off a cliff, and if [listeners are] ready to jump with me, we jump together, and it's another journey. The woman's journey: *Little Earthquakes* was the girl finding her voice, *Under the Pink* was testing those waters and looking primarily at women's relationships with women. This is a little volatile. About the men and what they gave me. Sometimes they gave me nothing and that was the gift. Sometimes they stood there and didn't come save me, didn't come make it okay, because at that point in a relationship when you're going your separate ways, you're on your own. It is a gift, being forced to claim your fire, but scary sometimes."

Speaking to *Billboard* in 1997, the year before her next album would be released, Tori Amos hinted that it would take a new direction: "It feels like *Earthquakes*, *Pink*, and *Pele* were a trilogy, and now a door has closed. A certain style ended for me. But as long as I honor wherever the music is going, whether or not radio plays it, then I think my audience will still be there. That is the most important thing to me."

"This record got me through a real bad patch. But I can laugh with this record, and I can move my hips to this record, which is really good for me."

— TORI AMOS (*NEXT*, 1999)

CHAPTER 6

From the Choirgirl Hotel
(1998)

Besides being a creative breakthrough, *Boys for Pele* brought Tori Amos closure on her breakup with Eric Rosse as well as a new personal relationship with sound engineer Mark Hawley. On tour in support of *Pele*, Tori became pregnant but had a miscarriage at the end of her first trimester, just before Christmas 1996. Though she had planned to take a break from writing and recording to be a mother, she now found herself in "no man's land" — not a mother, but not the person she was before her pregnancy. "It's strange," related Tori in a 1998 interview, "because I knew early on that I was pregnant — within days — so I got attached to it without really understanding the danger. I mean, I just didn't think that losing it was an option." Speaking to the *Chicago Tribune*, Tori identified the struggle she faced in the wake of her loss: "Just because death happens doesn't mean stuff stops. I think that was sort of the thing that happened when I miscarried. I was still very much on the planet, very much alive, but feeling that loss and not being able to find out where this spirit goes when it leaves the planet. What I found is that I'm not interested in saying, 'It's all for the best.' I'm just not interested in that put-a-ribbon-on-it crap. I'm okay with skinning my knees."

Reeling from the unexpected loss, Tori "went through a lot of different feelings after the miscarriage," she told *Jam*, "you go through everything possible. You question what is fair, you get angry with the spirit for not wanting to come, you keep asking why. And then, as I was going through the anger and the sorrow and the why, the songs started to come. Before I was even aware, they were coming to me in droves. Looking back, that's the way it's always happened for me in my life. When things get really empty for me — empty in my outer life — in my inner life, the music world, the songs come across galaxies to find me." She navigated her grief through music. Said Amos, "I spent hours a day working on the music. It wasn't a chore. It was a lifeline. It was about finding passion again, and being creative again. Being creative in a way that I could be. Creating some kind of life."

Though she had a hard time talking about the loss, she found freedom in her music. In an interview with the *Boston Globe*, she said, "I was trying to find strength as a woman somewhere — and it became this primal call, if you will, to the water. And to rhythm. It started to give the woman in me some kind of confidence, some kind of reason for being . . . I couldn't be a woman who was a mother. But I could be a woman who could hold a space for the songs. So that's what I chose to do at this time." Music was her only truly effective refuge, as the singer explained, "Crawling into the pain was the only way out." With these songs as with those on her previous three albums, Tori felt that they came to her from a muse or energy, which she had to channel and translate: "You have to open yourself to this energy. You have to learn how to tune your feelers. So, when you feel the muse coming, you can do something with it. It's kind of like tracking. Except you're hunting for something without a physical shape. It's located somewhere in the ether. And the trick is recognizing it. For that you have to learn to trust your feelings."

Not wanting to create a simple diary of what had happened to her in her songs, Tori instead "dug into" her wound, by taking a "flashlight into the confessional." Each song had a distinct personality and identity for Tori: "Every song is an individual. I call my songs 'girls' — in a way they have existed like the being who was at first outside of me, and then visited me, and then left because he/she couldn't settle. The songs are individuals, they visit me, I record them and then they go to the world by themselves. I send them away with a lunchbox and a juice bottle. Every girl has her own protons and neutrons inside her. 'Raspberry Swirl' is her own

unity and 'Spark' has a thing of her own . . . Later I started to see those girls at some hotel. Some of them spent time at the pool and drank margaritas. Some of them answered the phone after gagging the person at the reception. Another girl visited the strange guy at room number thirteen. I saw a bunch of people whose members were very independent yet they still worked together well. Sort of like a band. I wasn't sure about my role: would they let me join in, did they want me to tell what they were doing or were they trying to tell me things that I had to express." The *Choirgirl* songs told her, "'Tori, it's not just about you.'"

Uninterested in a series of songs that all sound the same, *From the Choirgirl Hotel* grew into an eclectic but united collection in terms of sound and subject matter. "Pandora's Aquarium" was the first song that came to her after she and Mark Hawley lost the baby, and as the writing process continued each song reflected a side to what Tori was going through. "So a song like 'Cruel' came to me out of my anger. 'She's Your Cocaine' and 'i i e e e' came out of a sense of loss and sacrifice. And other songs celebrated the fact that I found a new appreciation for life through this loss." The song "Northern Lad" dealt with "thinking you were loved for who you were, and realizing you weren't, and realizing maybe you don't love yourself. The line, 'I guess you go too far/ When pianos try to be guitars' is just about never being enough. I felt that with my instrument sometimes, wanting to be Jimmy Page. You can only be you. A lot of times it's never enough for people." One of the singles from the album, "Jackie's Strength," explored the idea of womanhood Jacqueline Kennedy presented: "I saw Jackie as a bride — and I used to think I would never be a bride. I started to look to Jackie and how that woman held the country together after she watched her husband get cut down right in front of her."

Amos became interested in rhythm on this album in a deeper way than she had been on previous records. One catalyst came via a dance remix of "Professional Widow": "I made a very obscure record last time and Johnny D, a DJ friend of mine in New York, said, 'Hey, it would be great if you did a few dance remixes' and suggested this guy van Helden. It was that simple — nobody thought anything would happen with it. I certainly didn't think it would become, like, a benchmark in dance music . . . What it did for me though was it inspired me to open up my thinking to rhythm — to use rhythm in a different way." Amos felt that exploring beyond the "girl and her piano" foundation was important for her growth as a musician. She told the *Washington Post*, "Playing by myself for so many years, doing so many shows, I thought maybe I was hiding behind myself at the piano . . . I felt like it was time to bring in real players, real rhythm. It's such a magical thing when a group of people can groove together, and I wanted to plug in to this ancient place where the banshees go. There can be beauty and ballads there, but it can also grab you by the throat."

Providing a glimpse into her writing process for the album, Tori Amos revealed to *Keyboard*, "I wrote a lot of it at the keyboard but also at the synth, too. . . . The good thing is they maxed me out at Kurzweil with sounds, and then my friend came in and gave me a bunch of sounds — Mellotron sounds and stuff, 'tron viola, 'tron flute, 'tronny stuff like that. I started messing with them and in some cases writing things around some of them, like in 'Hotel.' So the keyboard was very present while I was writing. I wrote most everything before I walked into the studio." Just as the harpsichord had moved to center stage on *Boys for Pele*, for *Choirgirl*, Tori's Kurzweil helped shape the songs.

The recording of the album took place in an old converted barn in Cornwall, England. Engineer Marcel van Limbeek recalled, "*Choirgirl* was a whole challenge in and of itself. Like *Boys for Pele*, *Choirgirl* was a challenge because we built that studio, believe it or not, in seven or eight weeks from when they decided to do it and Mark bought the place, 'til about two months later when we had to start recording in there, so it was pretty stressful to do." Tori loved working in the 300-year-old barn: "The great thing about being away from a music-industry city is that people can't just pop by — that's the first thing. It's really important for me to have freedom, and when you're in London or in L.A. or in New York recording, the access is just so easy. It's too easy for comfort, really. Being outside of a major city, for me, has always been desirable."

The studio, which came to be called Martian Engineering, was constructed with Amos's particular recording needs in mind. Explained van Limbeek, "Our design definitely related to her style of playing because she plays acoustic instruments, so when I'm speaking about comb filtering and minimizing that in the recording room as much as in the mix room, it's equally as important, but will matter more if you work with acoustic instruments. If you record electronic stuff and programmed stuff, it matters for a mixing room but not for a recording room. But in Tori's case, the heart of her music has always been her Bösendorfer piano; it's a big, acoustic thing with loads and loads of harmonics. So the acoustic sound has always been very important to her." The studio's control room was designed so Steve Caton, who was back as guitarist on the album, and the bass player could play there as Tori and the drummer, Matt Chamberlain, played live in their separate rooms.

The idea of having the programmer and gear along with musicians together in the control room had originated during production on *Boys for Pele*. Van Limbeek recalled, "It had originally struck us — in terms of the control room size — that when we were looking for a mix room to mix *Boys for Pele*, as we traveled through England to listen to different studios, we were struck by how completely different the control rooms sounded. How colored they were sounding, and that really worried us, because it became a question of 'What do you do?' So we started buying books and reading up on things like comb filtering, and basically came up with this design. It became our philosophy to come up with a control room that had a reflection-free zone behind the board to stop any sort of direct reflections from interfering with the direct signal coming out of the speakers, to avoid comb filtering basically. So the design of the room is one where you had symmetrical but non-parallel walls and a slope ceiling, so any sort of reflections off the side walls or the ceiling will be reflected to the back of the room. And the back of the room is basically one big diffuser, or half diffuser and half absorber, and so by the time reflections do hit your ear, they'll be coming from the back wall, but nicely diffused rather than hard reflections from the wall. So you get a cleaner sound basically."

"*Choirgirl* had a more proper recording environment for sure," opined Marcel van Limbeek, "because [it] was the first time Mark and Tori basically built their own studio [with] a big room where Tori could have her imperial-sized Bösendorfer piano that's surrounded by God-knows-what-else she might fancy playing at the time: from organs to harpsichords to clavichords to electronic keyboards. . . . We ended up with two really big rooms next to each other: the main recording room — which if you were recording strings, I'd say you could house up to twenty people — and the main recording room that had the Neve console. Then off to the side there were four smaller rooms for recording anything else at the same time. So from a recording point of view, you'd say it's a medium-sized studio, but from a mixing point of view, it's a major-sized studio, because the control room is brilliant, very spacious."

Rhythm was a more important component on this album than ever before for Tori, and Mark Hawley and Marcel van Limbeek impressed upon her that if she wanted to capture the sound she was after, she would need to cut the tracks live. Said Tori to *Inside Connection*, "I wanted to capture a certain atmosphere that was only possible with drums, not with additional drums but with real life drums. I needed the interaction with a drummer. I want to grow, personally and musically, and to grow you have to move on, you have to experiment, otherwise it becomes far too static . . . I let the rhythm take over, it wasn't really easy because I'm a control freak, but I thought if I want good rhythms then I have to feel them, get caught up in them. This is the first album I recorded with a live percussionist, the first album where there was interaction with other musicians. Usually I recorded the vocals, the piano, and the rest of the instruments were somehow placed around it." Eric Rosse suggested to Tori that she try out Matt Chamberlain for the gig, and within the first few minutes of playing together, it was obvious that they were a perfect fit. Said the singer, "I met with him and played with him and my jaw just dropped to the floor. Wow, psychic rhythm!"

Matt Chamberlain related how he came to work on *Choirgirl* . . . and every album Tori's recorded since: "I met Tori through Eric Rosse, and he had produced a couple of records by another band of mine, and during that time he'd said Tori had contacted him wanting to get more rhythmic, and have a drummer be more a part of the basic tracks when she was recording the record. So he got me in contact with Tori, and we chatted on the phone, and she asked me if I wanted to come out to her place in Florida, set up a drum kit in her living room, and play. So I flew down there, and rented a drum kit, and literally just set it up in her living room next to her PA. This was right before *Choirgirl Hotel*, so she played me a bunch of demos from that record. She had a little Mackie and a TASCAM 88 set up next to her piano there, and we put a mic up on the drum kit and played some songs down. I think she recorded them, and we just ended up doing that over the weekend and had a great time. So when I got back to Seattle after that experience, she called a second time and said, 'Hey, do you want to come out to Cornwall and do a record?' And of course, I was overly excited to do that."

For Tori, the recording process changed with Chamberlain's presence. As she told *Wall of Sound*, "It became about a conversation. The drums would pull one way, and the piano would pull another. A relationship was happening on tape. The voice was working off a hi-hat, possibly, or was pushing something, pulling back. Then the kick [drum] pattern would change, and therefore my left hand would move differently, which would make the bass player do something different. So that's the way we did it — based around live performance and waiting around until the muse showed up."

The conversational approach to crafting *From the Choirgirl Hotel* marked a shift in Amos's career. After the songs were written, she communicated to the musicians and engineers her image of the track in her own inimitable manner: "I would say, 'Okay, imagine this girl as completely made of a frozen lake. I want you to imagine a drill — one of those long motherfuckers — coming right into her. The thing, though, is that she doesn't bleed blood. She's transparent, and yet she is in physical form. And I want to hear that in these eight bars.' And they would make me go away for a few hours so I wouldn't bug them. It was about getting the musicians to really hear the soul of the song, and then giving them freedom. That entails a certain amount of letting go, after you've had nearly full control over every sound on your albums in the past. It became very much about what instrument is the guiding, anchored force that's taking us through the rabbit hole right now. Sometimes it would be: 'No, this is all about the guitar, so forget about everybody else. Mute this and keep that.' You can't be overly precious about, 'Well, I played this and I worked really hard.' Well, so what? It's not about this — it's about the bass line for two bars. Mute the piano."

Comparing the approach on the previous album to this one, van Limbeek suggested, "On *Boys for Pele*, we'd made this record where we just tried to downplay all the production on it, so that the musicianship would shine through. We kept it safe with as many high quality units doing as little as possible. So it was all about the music, and as little about any trickery. On *Choirgirl Hotel*, in many ways we tried to do the opposite, to get away from that. So we worked with Andy Gray, he was a programmer who introduced Pro Tools to us, and it all became about fancy sounds. We started using filters a lot more, coming up with lo-fi sounds — so it was a totally, totally different record, combined with recording it in a brand new studio we'd built ourselves." Mark Hawley explained to *Sound on Sound* one of reasons for the change from *Pele* to *Choirgirl*: "[T]he last album was quite a classical sounding thing and a very personal project for Tori. It did extremely well in the States and it will always be one of my favorites, but the record company was rather unsure about it. I guess it was not too great on radio because it was so dynamic, and so this time we decided to make a bit of a pop album."

Hawley revealed one of Amos's strengths as a producing partner: "Tori is a pure musician and isn't interested in the technical aspects, but the great thing about working with her is that she is never unsure about anything. She will make a decision and will say when something is right. A lot of artists are quick to say when something is wrong, but Tori will say when it is right too, and you know when she says that, it is right, and she won't change her mind again. A lot of musicians like Tori find it very hard to listen to a mix as you are building it up, and not automatically hear [that mix as if it were] the finished thing, so although we might be quite happy with a quick reverb slapped on the vocal, and a rough drum reverb as we are building the mix, whenever Tori walks in she hears it as the finished thing." Agreed van Limbeek, "Timing is everything in terms of when she listens to the mixes."

Of working with the band, which enabled her to become a different kind of piano player, Tori said she'd found the best musicians she could. Discussing her dynamic with the band to the *Detroit Free Press*, Amos gushed, "I love these players. It's always about encouraging other people. They know that I can have two heads — a conceptual arranger's head, and then the artist's head. And sometimes I have to put the artist aside, because what she's doing maybe isn't as good as what the bass player is doing. My commitment is to the best choice. Obviously, somebody's got to make the final decision of 'This lick is better here' or 'This groove is better here,' but I think the musicians and engineers feel a lot of freedom. . . . The main thing I want is that the players feel challenged as players, and, number two, that they're always thinking about the soul of a song. I obviously picked players who aren't about having to make a piece the way they want to make it. We're not U2. That's not what this is. They have a certain respect from me, and they know that's why they're here." To *Musician*, Tori explained the advantage of her background when it comes to working with a band: "I'm a player. I'm not solely a singer. And I feel for some of the girls who just sing but are very dependent on players. They may be talented, but they're not musicians. Some of them are good songwriters and good collaborators with other players. They have a gift, but you cannot command respect of seasoned players — it's very difficult . . . You can't rest on your laurels. You have to understand rhythm and you need to know how to communicate with those drummers. You need to explain what you need." Learning how to work with other musicians Tori found she had to separate parts of herself — as both a producer and as an artist — in order to create the best possible working and creative relationships.

From Matt Chamberlain's perspective, Tori Amos is "a really unique artist in that she likes to experiment, or at least she likes to do drastically different things on every record. So she'll set up scenarios for you as a musician: for *Choirgirl Hotel*, it was more of 'Let's get real rhythmic, and bring a programmer in.' So she brought in Andy Gray, who I'd never worked with before. And at the time, Pro Tools was kicking in big time, and so I was really excited about playing grooves into Andy Gray's Pro Tools rig, and then having him mangulate the drums. Run the drums through filters, and all the plug-ins that were available, and basically treat me as a loop CD. Like have me be a source of beats, where we made up a bunch of beats organically, and record them into Pro Tools. With Tori, since she'd usually been such a solo artist, she tends to cover everything with what she plays, so that she's a full-on rhythm section with just herself. So you can throw down some drums with her, just playing piano, and get everything you need. That's the hard part of being a bass player with her is she'll play a lot of the stuff that, as a bass player, you'd probably play anyway, so you have to figure out how to fit in around that. As a drummer, I tend to play to her groove over that of the bassist.

"The crazy thing about Tori is when you're recording with her — the traditional way of doing records now is that you go in with the intent of just getting a basic track, the rhythm section. Then usually what happens is the vocalist and all the overdubs get done after you get the basic tracks, and the vocalist will spend time doing different takes, that are then comped together to get a great performance. Tori will actually get her vocals and her piano part with the drum track, which is *crazy*, if you think about it — it's insane. She's getting it in real time with you, and she might fix a few little words here and there, but her vocals are done when you're overdubbing the shaker on the basic tracks; her vocals are already done, it's amazing. On *Choirgirl*, she'd let me pretty much go nuts, because the whole idea on that record had been 'Let's get a drummer in and get rhythmic, and really feature some rhythms on this.' So when it came time to do the tour, it just made sense to give me a call, because we'd created it together, and there was no way she'd just call some Joe Blow session guy to go on the road. We'd had such a great time doing it, and just hit it off. She's not that type of person generally either; she sticks with the same people for everything, really, which is pretty amazing."

In an interview with *Sound on Sound*, van Limbeek detailed the technical side of the recording sessions: "[W]e still used the U 87s on some tracks, but we also used AKG C 414s because they make the Bösendorfer sound much more like a 'pop' piano. It sounds slightly smaller, but it doesn't sound brittle, and it sits better in the mix with the drums and the rest of the band. We also tried using a U 87 on the low end and a C 414 on the high end to get a really great blend of warmth and brightness, which worked very well on some tracks." For Tori, her Bösendorfer is in "another league than the other [pianos]. She's handmade, and we got her MIDIed up so I can play with a band without all the feedback and stuff. If you played her, you would understand. Just in the action, the way she talks back to you as an instrument. She talks back in a different way."

For Tori's vocals, it was important for Hawley and van Limbeek to distinguish between the moments when she sang from her stomach versus from her throat; understanding that, said Hawley, allowed them to get a lot more from the recordings. Van Limbeek revealed how those vocals were captured by detailing their microphone choices: "A mic which sounded beautiful on Tori's voice that we used quite a bit was the Sony C-37A; it's a gorgeous sounding mic. Another mic we kept that M 49 and perhaps the U 87, but the Sony was the main mic we used. Her drummer Matt Chamberlain had brought it in, and we first used it on the snare, but then we started using it on Tori's vocals and started tracking quite a few songs with that. What we all liked about that mic especially was its character. It's a tonal thing, there's a beautiful midrange, and so for some songs, it would just make you cry. It's not at all the most precise microphone, but there's quite a bit of character to it definitely." Touching on mic separation, Mark Hawley said to *Sound on Sound*, "I think you can go too far in trying to get everything completely separate, and there is a danger that you might lose the ambient sound of the room. A bit of crosstalk is perfectly okay, so with this album we used a simple soundboard which went over the front of the piano to provide a degree of screening. We still had some crosstalk between the voice and piano, but at least it was reflected rather than direct sound."

As for the recording setup with "brilliant" guitarist Steve Caton, van Limbeek described it as fairly simple: "He would design his sound in a bunch of pedals and use a stereo processor too. Steve was great, he totally designed his own sound, and sometimes we amped it up, and sometimes he just ran directly out of his box. In terms of dealing with him, it was easy for us because he gave us a complete full sound, and that was it. The only thing you had to do was bring the phaser up and it sounded great." Amos had known Caton since she was 21 and described their musical relationship as having both chemistry and magic: "[He] has a very fluid, ambient style of guitar playing that's very subtle. It sneaks in and kind of wraps around a lot of the songs."

Some tracks on *Choirgirl* required additional instrumentation; for "Jackie's Strength," Tori's piano was wheeled out to make room for a 15-piece string section, remembers van Limbeek. "So the miking approach we used for all the string sections on that album is a main stereo pair of omni-directional DPA 4003s. There's something about using those as a stereo pair with Tori's music; her voice always sits so in the middle of it, it's the main thing. To mix in strings nicely with it using those 4003s always works really well basically. When you work with A/Bs, instead of X/Y or M/Ss, you might have more of a hole in the middle, but that's exactly then where Tori fits. So we did that, then in addition using a main stereo pair, which is what will likely be up for seventy percent of the mix; we'll also use spot mics on all the instruments as well. So for instance, all the first violins will have one microphone, all the second violins will have one spot microphone over it, and then the same with the viola and the cellos."

On the simpler side was the miking for drummer Matt Chamberlain, who saw the setup and thought, "'Wow, these guys just use your basic old mics on drums.' For overheads, Marcel was using AKG 414s and the kick was an AKG D 112, a Shure 57 on the snare drum. It was real simple mics you see even in rock clubs; [it] wasn't anything esoteric for the *Choirgirl Hotel* record. They had some really nice mics for the piano and vocals, but at the time, the studio was just being finished. I mean, they had just built it. So they didn't have the usual mics that you get spoiled with doing sessions in really great studios that have been around forever. And that wasn't really the idea for that record anyway. The idea was to capture the drums live, and then tweak them out in Pro Tools. Some of the drum kits I used on *Choirgirl* were not traditional drum kits. I had a kit that was made out of percussion instruments, and all the percussion instruments would be arranged in a way where it was familiar for me to play as a drummer. So where the bass drum would usually be, I'd put a low-toned instrument, and where the snare drum would be would be a higher-pitched thing, so I could make beats out of that. So the idea of doing that kind of thing was so exciting to me because I love that. I love experimenting, and I'm a big fan of electronic music and experimental stuff that has a lot of beats in it." Elaborating on the drum setup, van Limbeek explained, "We also changed the acoustics of the room to make it more dead sometimes. It really all depended on the kind of sound we wanted for the music, and what the rack was all about."

For Tori, the emphasis on rhythm had to be an organic part of the song, evident especially in *Choirgirl*'s "Raspberry Swirl." Amos reasoned, "[I]f I'm going to write a song, I don't want to just put rhythm on top of it, I want to write a rhythm into it, so it's part of the architecture. ['Cruel' is] not just written as a ballad at the piano and then you come up with a catchy rhythm." Matt Chamberlain added, "['Cruel'] was more chopped up and pieced together in Pro Tools, more collage or construction pieces. But the stuff that really sticks out for me is more of the performance stuff where we actually had to play together. That would include songs like 'Black Dove,' 'Playboy Mommy,' 'Pandora's Aquarium,' which were more of a fun experience because we played together, and it happened fairly quickly. In one or two takes and we'd be done."

Choirgirl Hotel took only six months from start to finish; principal tracking began on September 8 and the album was in stores by May of the following year. Of the mixing process, Hawley revealed to *Sound on Sound* that while Amos is not that involved in the nitty gritty, she provides inspiration to the engineers: "Tori loves art and photography, and I remember . . . in the lounge of the studio, she was going over some art book, and she looked at a picture, and she showed it to me and Mark, and said, 'Think of that when you're mixing that song.' Sometimes we do that still, we look at art when we mix. Another routine we have is that we always light a candle when we put a mix down." Helping expedite the process was a database created by studio technician Rob van Tuin that logs everything recorded during each session, allowing easier access to particular takes.

Landing on *Spin*'s top albums of 1998 list, *From the Choirgirl Hotel* charted in the U.S., the U.K., across Europe, and Australia, and earned her a Grammy nomination for Best Alternative Music Album, an honor she'd received for *Pele* and *Under the Pink* as well. "Raspberry Swirl" also picked up a nomination for Female Rock Vocal Performance. For Amos, most importantly, the process of creating the album had helped her through her grief. Reflecting on how her personal tragedy shaped *From the Choirgirl Hotel*, Amos said, "I'm sure if I would have become a mother that it still would have been a valid record. A different record, but a valid one. And maybe some day I'll have that experience. I think what I write about happens to a lot of people: somebody is devastated by the breakup of a marriage. They are on the brink and brought to their knees. People go through crises all the time — the loss of a job, a friendship dissolves. I think life brings different losses. Some are turning points in your life, some go quietly in the night."

"The concept that there are albums
that make you happy and albums that
make you suicidal — I don't live in that
kind of segregated world."

— TORI AMOS (*USA TODAY*, 1999)

CHAPTER 7

To Venus and Back
(1999)

Heading into the new millennium, Tori Amos was ready for a break after years of tirelessly recording and touring. Her plan was to release a live album and a disc of rarities and unreleased tracks, and then spend the summer "hang[ing] out at [her] beach house." But *To Venus and Back* ended up with an album's worth of new material as well as the "best performances" from her *Choirgirl* tour. Explained Tori, "At the time, I was writing stuff, thinking I was gonna pick three songs [to put on the album], and having the B-sides sent in from all reaches of the land. And we were going to remix everything, because it needed a bit of a tart-up, especially the B-sides. Some of them were done very quickly, and not with the best care. . . . As I played these new songs to my producers, what they said to me was, theoretically speaking, this will sound like a random hodgepodge of bits and pieces, because sonically, the new work lives in a world by itself. I just looked at them and said, 'N-n-n-no. What are you guys saying?' And they said, 'This is a record unto itself, and you really can't break it up. It doesn't work geometrically.'" Not wanting to release a "hodgepodge" and with new songs coming fast and furious to her, Tori Amos unexpectedly and unintentionally had an album of new material in the works.

It had been arranged for Matt Chamberlain to fly in and record the few new tracks at Martian Engineering in Cornwall. As Tori told the *Los Angeles Times*, she "called up Matt and said, 'Before you get on the plane, just one thing. We're cutting thirteen [tracks], not three.' And we had the same amount of time to do it in." Chamberlain was game: "While *Venus* was just going to be a live record, she'd also been writing on the road, and we'd all obviously been playing tons together. So she thought it would be fun to go into the studio and capture whatever it is we'd been doing together. So the idea was just to record a few songs, and it turned out to be a little bit more than just a few of her songs. She's just one of those artists — I don't understand where it all comes from — but she's a non-stop songwriter."

The album's title was inspired by an evening Tori spent with her girlfriends drinking wine. As she related to vh1, "[My friend] Natalie was the one who looked at me and said, 'You'd go to Venus if you could.' And I said, 'Wherever that is.' Of course, we know the planet — and we're all looking galactic because of where we're going — but there's also the mythology of Venus, which is the feminine. So it just came to me." With the title decided upon, the songs followed. Unlike with past projects, the writing was not completely finished before entering her home studio to record. Tori endeavored to show all the sides of Venus that came to her: "[I]t was almost as if the songs from Venus decided to say, 'These are fragments of Venus she's willing to show you at this time,' and I felt like I climbed up on this little satellite and started roaming around her heart." In terms of her state of mind while composing the songs for *Venus*, Tori told *USA Today*, "After the Plugged tour, I sort of walked into a fierce calm. I didn't need to be someone's daughter, wife, or mother — even though I am a daughter and a wife, and motherhood kind of just slipped through time and space for me. The record is just about being a woman and waking up every day."

Of her approach as a lyricist, Tori explained to *All Music*, "You have to journey with [the parables]. I give you perspectives from where I wrote it. They take on their own life forms. But there's word association, and sometimes I give people the bloodline. It gives you a character study of who she is. But then she has a whole subtext to her that's going on, that some people read into her and I haven't. But I never write it to be literal, until I choose to. If I want to be literal, I'll be literal. But when you're on a datura trip, you don't do it to be literal. The literal bit of it is the garden: it's very factual, being read, doing a roll call."

To Venus and Back explored darkness — "the shadows and the shadow world" — and Tori envisioned each song as its own short film. "Juarez" was based on the murders of hundreds of women in Juarez, Mexico, while "Datura" takes its name from the plant that is used by some as a hallucinogen. "Bliss" explored the idea of patriarchal control, whether religious or familial. "1000 Oceans" came to Tori in the night, a voice singing her the melody; she rose early and recorded a piece of the melody into the tape recorder she keeps by her piano in the studio, then worked to craft the full track from it. The song "became about feeling close to people you can't reach, seeing this depth of love for this person who was gone." The decadence of the 1980s and the vitality and vision of the art world that Tori felt was now gone fueled "Glory of the 80s." In "Suede," seduction and blame twisted with obsession and passion; says Amos of the song, "she knows what she's up to; she knows what she's been doing."

"Bliss" and "Concertina" in different ways dealt with the idea of those outside oneself imposing their will. In an interview with *Alternative Press*, Tori discussed the genesis of these feelings: "When I was growing up, I started becoming very secretive about my thoughts and the sensory world I would go to, because there's a lot of mind control that goes on constantly. People wanting to access: 'What are you thinking?' So sometimes I'd have my own defense going, which would be to look them straight in the eye and make them think I've killed my imagination. But it's like, I'll take control."

Marcel van Limbeek, photographed during Tori's Sinful Attraction tour.

Just as the writing came fast and furious, so did the recording. As she told *Wall of Sound*, "This is the fastest one we've ever done. Sometimes it just takes you longer to do something; you can't hear it or see it, and you're kind of half-present. But we were very tweaked, and we were very present, and this record was demanding us to be very present. She was so seductive none of us could sleep — none of us wanted to. It was like some Dionysian frenzy. We didn't want to stop. It was a fierce calm." Mark Hawley told *Alternative Press* that "the whole new album was so relaxed when we were recording it, the vibe was incredible. It sounds corny, but that comes through on the record."

Marking an evolutionary step stylistically from *Choirgirl*, the new material on *To Venus and Back* had to complement the live tracks. Said Amos, "*Venus* is very much about sound effects. . . . She's of the ether, so sonically and lyrically, the sound of her is very — it's the extreme from the live record. The live record has no overdubs to it . . . the guys tarted her up a lot, but it's about having been there, and the principles are different at work for a live record that is of the third dimension than a work that's coming from Venus, which is really from the ether trying to materialize here on Earth in this space." Tori came to the music from an emotional place where her sound engineers came from a theoretical one: "Things have to add up geometrically for the engineers. I mean, they're not just guys who play with buttons. Engineering is their life passion. A lot of things were designed — effects were designed — by hand. We were playing with EQs and compression, using compression as an instrument, taking it to new levels for me . . . If we were using a program, it had to be right for the character [of the song]." In that vein, guitarist Steve Caton offered, "I really love what I do with Tori. I'm no amateur caught up in a frenzy of technique, nor am I the type that goes for an avalanche of notes. I'm interested in the texture of sounds. . . . I would say that she leaves me ninety-nine percent free to play how I want. There are so many parts where the guitars don't sound like guitars. Some people tell me, 'I listened to this album you play on, but I never heard you!' And I tell them that I do appear on it, but that what I do is 'non-guitaristic.'"

Comparing the albums from a technical perspective, Marcel van Limbeek suggested, "With *Boys for Pele*, it was all audiophile, doing as little as possible if you like, and in the mix too, there's very little going on. What is going on is high quality, and with *Choirgirl Hotel*, there was a lot more trickery. So with *Venus*, we were maybe going one step back from *Choirgirl Hotel*. We were still very much in the process of fine-tuning the studio too, you know. With *Choirgirl Hotel*, we walked into this brand new space, and we didn't have any chance to test if out. So after we did that record and tour, me and Mark went straight back into the studio to make *Venus*. And I remember we made a few small but crucial changes to the control room, added some extra absorption in there, and some extra diffusion in the live room. I'm sure those changes to the studio came across in the album as well. In terms of equipment too, I remember we definitely bought some hi-quality EQ, we got this

Massenburg EQ at the time." Andy Gray was back to assist with the programming, with Tori playing on his PPG Waveform. "Sometimes I'd be playing synth with one hand and piano with the other. I love that kind of amalgamating," Tori told *All Music*. "For the most part, we're developing a theme from ourselves in our own loops ... [On] 'Glory of the 80s,' I love some of the Minimoogs and those old sounds, and also the new sounds. What I have a hard time with is a lot of electronica. I don't like a lot of it, because it's real cheesy, [from] people who don't know keyboard sounds, not just the sounds, but the choice of the notes with the sound; that's so fundamental. It's not just the sound, but how you use the sound. Rather than rely on sequencing to pound out a dance beat, you bring your micromanaging aesthetic to the technology. On 'Glory of the 80s' you drop a quick synth gliss behind the words, 'the end is nothing to fear.' Whether phrasing a vocal line or using electronic tools, you're still aware of the details." Again for "Concertina," Tori knew what feeling behind the sounds she needed to capture: "I wanted those electronic drums that Matt was playing with because particle by particle, she slowly changes, and I wanted the sense of the acoustic piano with the electronic drums. That also reoccurs in 'Lust.' So there was this dichotomy going on and I'm really drawn to that."

To achieve the right sound for *Venus*, drummer Matt Chamberlain brought in vintage drum kits: "I just wanted to get more character out of the drums. An acoustic guitar player will have certain acoustic guitars because they have a certain character, so when you're recording acoustic drums, you're looking for that. You don't necessary want the newest, most bland-sounding drum kit. You want something with a little bit of tone and vibe to it, so that's what I was trying to go for with that [1960s Gretsch kit]. And it's become generally what I try to go for with most records. Her music is so different for every record; for *Venus*, we tracked the album fairly fast. On one of the album's songs, 'Datura,' for instance, we got to record two different drum kits going through these enveloped filters panned hard left and right. When the groove kicks in, it's two different drum kits, one coming out of the left speaker and one out of the right, processed through these meter petals [enveloped filters], that made the drums sound like blasters. That was

Mark Hawley, photographed during Tori's Sinful Attraction tour.

a standout moment for sure, because it was so bizarre and I couldn't believe she was going to put it on her record. I thought, 'That's insane!'"

The vintage drum kit wasn't the only piece of equipment Chamberlain brought into the studio for the recording of *To Venus and Back*: "I'd brought in a few more pieces of gear, because I'm a total studio gear freak. So I brought out an old Telefunken U 47, which was an old classic tube mic. If you go way back into the history of that mic, it was developed by the Germans during World War II to make Hitler's voice sound like God, that, unfortunately and fortunately, was the idea. It's just a beautiful sounding, full frequency, tube condenser microphone that enhances anything that sounds good; that mic just makes it sound better.

"So during the session, we placed it in front of the kit to capture a general picture of the drum kit, which was then mixed in with all the other closer mics. I also brought two Coles Ribbon mics, which were developed by the BBC for recording orchestras back in the forties and are just really beautiful mics that we used for overheads. For the kick drum, we used an AKG D 12, and I also used a Sony C-37A tube mic, which is like the U 47 in that it's a really nice sounding, full frequency microphone. The thing you look for in mics when recording drums is to give you a nice picture, sort of like in photography when they talk about the lenses, which make pictures look a certain way. So the C-37A is just a great mic you can put on almost anything, but we decided to put it on the snare drum. We ended up using that C-37A on the vocal mic too, because it sounded so great. Marcel was curious of how it would sound, grabbed it, and they were just all blown away by it."

Van Limbeek added, on the subject of microphones, "We definitely asked Matt to come back with the Sony C-37A, that's for sure, and used the same U 87 on the piano. I think what was different for the drums on *Venus*, for overhead mics we used Coles Ribbon mics. Again, Matt turned up with those, and then we bought our own. We liked them because they're less bright and softer sounding, and beautiful on cymbals, a real specific lush sound. So we used those on the drum sounds. Also, we had a bromaline configuration over the drum kit, basically two [figure of eight] ribbon mics, and if you have them right next to each other — like X/Y — but at an angle of ninety degrees, then you have a pick-up pattern that's called bromaline. It's a technique that comes from early stereo recording, and we used that for the drum overheads, and got a really, really lush sound."

With both Mark Hawley and Marcel van Limbeek working sound on Amos's tours as well as the studio recordings, they had gotten into the practice of running a DAT to record her during soundchecks, because Tori often likes to try out new songs or compose instead of doing a strict soundcheck for the upcoming performance. Says van Limbeek of the live show setup, "Since our earliest shows, we've always multi-tracked it, and me and Mark were the first ones to set that up. Nowadays, you have the digital mixing desks, and with them, it's fairly easy if you combine them with hard disk recording systems. We were doing that in 1994, multi-track recording every single show, and every soundcheck as well. So if Tori ever had an idea, or comes up with a new song, we can just multi-track record at any time." Choosing the live tracks for *To Venus and Back* meant reviewing a lot of recordings. Explained the singer, "We did over a hundred and twenty gigs last year, and I listened to every one of them and we ranked them and rated them in a play-off." Matt Chamberlain explained some of the criteria used for the "play-off": "We all had to find a performance where we were all playing correctly . . . The versions of the songs we did live were different than on the record, which made them unique. 'Waitress,' for example, is a nine-minute space jam that's totally different from the version on the record. Tori wanted to have stuff on the live record that the live band transformed." Songs that held a "soft spot" for a member of the team made it on: Amos and van Limbeek selecting "Bells for Her," and Hawley, "Space Dog."

Regarding the technical side of putting the tracks together — live and newly recorded — van Limbeek explained, "On *Venus*, it was the first record we actually recorded into Pro Tools; we ditched the tape machine and went straight into Pro Tools. So the live portion of *Venus* was all recorded using remote pre-amps, and the Neve was used for monitoring and later on for mixing. Live, I would have a few plate reverbs, pre-programmed, that were always good for her to use. I always have three reverbs that are based upon vocal plates that are in the 480. I've got them ready to go just in case she starts doing a song I've never heard before. So within the first few seconds, I make my mind up as to which I think is appropriate. The reverbs vary in size from a small, medium, and a bigger one, and usually what we do is, as she's singing, I'll fine-tune the size and the amount of high-end, and the pre-delay, all depending on the tempo of the song, and the sound of the mic itself, of course. So that was always our starting-off point for recording live."

Identifying the pair's greatest challenge in the course of road recording, Mark Hawley quipped, "You don't come across nine-foot Bösendorfer pianos on live tours a lot, and we asked everyone for ideas on how to deal with it. We tried everything — all the usual bugs and pick-ups — but nothing worked as well as the classic studio technique of a pair of good cardioid mics. The whole idea of the bugs is to try to get rid of the ambient noise on the stage, but a lot of that is picked up directly by the piano itself — the sound board resonates in sympathy. With the piano lid open it can pick up so much ambient sound that before the show has started the piano mic channel meters on the desk would often be peaking up to the top just with the audience noise! We found if the ambient noise is already in the piano, using a pair of mics like Neumann U 87s gives you a much better sound quality than all the bugs."

Once she'd turned in the new LP, Tori told CNN that in her process of letting go at the end of any recording session, "There's always something on every album that I wished had slipped through. This album has just gone to the glass master. It's just down the street with its lunch box, although it has a bottle of Krug in it. I wouldn't be releasing it if I weren't happy with it, but if you talk to me nine months from now, there will be other things I'll have discovered." Debuting at #12 on the Billboard Top 200 Album chart, the double disc earned Tori Amos her fifth and sixth Grammy nominations. *Rolling Stone*'s favorable review described the album as "ornate, [and] flush with technology: mystery-ridden keyboardscapes and sample-and-loop witchery. Amos's stock in trade, her voice and piano, are often mere bit players on *Venus* . . . With *To Venus and Back*, Amos pays herself the ultimate compliment: She's good and complicated."

"I didn't know that these words from men would take hold of me. I thought I'd find out something about them. Instead, I found something out about myself."

— TORI AMOS (*ELLE*, 2001)

CHAPTER 8

Strange Little Girls (2001)

Tori's next studio album was, like those before it, shaped by an event in her personal life: the birth of her daughter, Natashya. Being a mother to an infant meant slowing down the constant touring and working, a good change for Amos. To *Woman's Journal*, she said, "I had three miscarriages before she was born, so she's very precious. As a musician you spend a lot of time traveling and living in hotels, so when we get a chance to breathe, we want to make our own food and sit on our own porch and just play house. I love being a hermit."

Tori found herself listening to the radio more often and in hearing the male artists' music, she began thinking about the gender divide and how men view women. Explained Tori to *Performing Songwriter*, "Words can wound and words can heal, and both are included on [*Strange Little Girls*]. A person has to take responsibility for their words. We as writers cannot separate ourselves from what we create. All of these songs were created by powerful wordsmiths, whether you agree with them or not . . . Even though I have love for some of [the men], and respect for some of the writers, the project was more about how men say things and what a woman hears, which led me to how men say things and what a man hears, which led me to songs that resonate with men, not songs I thought did. So I fondly called this 'the laboratory of men.' It became this forum and this research group for kicking around all sorts of thoughts." A concept album was born: *Strange Little Girls* featured Amos covering songs written exclusively by male artists.

Approached from a place of fascination rather than anger or frustration, Tori chose "powerful songs written by male artists, each one has its own unique story and voice, and I wanted to try and inject a female voice and expression to them. It does not come from an interest in the particular artists; it is the message, passion and power of the songs." She selected songs by The Velvet Underground ("New Age"), Eminem ("'97 Bonnie & Clyde"), The Stranglers ("Strange Little Girl"), Depeche Mode ("Enjoy the Silence"), 10cc ("I'm Not in Love"), Lloyd Cole ("Rattlesnakes"), Tom Waits ("Time"), Neil Young ("Heart of Gold"), The Boomtown Rats ("I Don't Like Mondays"), The Beatles ("Happiness Is a Warm Gun"), Slayer ("Raining Blood"), and Joe Jackson ("Real Men"). Just as she did in her own original songs, in each of these Tori saw a personality, the titular "strange little girls." Said Tori, "Let's look at this a little more closely. Let's crawl behind the men's eyes and hang in their heads. And then let them crawl back over that bridge into the skins of these different women and see how they heard what they had written. You take the man's seed, you plant it in the womb of the voice of the woman, and the consummation happens there. This album has a Y chromosome in it."

Of course, Amos's teenage years spent covering songs in Georgetown bars, and her continued tradition of covering material during live performances, made the concept a perfect fit for her. To the *Boston Globe*, Tori revealed the unusual relationship she had with the material: "It's not about your own work, where your DNA is in your songs and you are the mom. This is something I really had to approach differently. You have to acknowledge that these men are the song mothers. I'm not the mother here. But what I did find surprising was that with each male song, a different female character came intrinsically tied to it that had access to me."

Her process of selecting the songs began with her "control group" of men whom she consulted about the material. Explained Tori, "We saw very different pictures of it and I was very influenced by a couple of the men and how the songs affected them — so there's many layers to this: not just the songwriters and their versions, but there's the men that brought the songs and their stories and their opinions of us. . . . Sometimes I disagree virulently with them. Sometimes I sat back and said, 'Okay, I see how they're affected,' but then I'd see the female character."

To transform each of the artists' songs into her own interpretation of it, Tori had to analyze the songs in a way that she hadn't done before, despite having sung countless cover versions throughout her life. "I had to deconstruct [the songs] if I was really going to make this project what I hoped it would become," she told *Performing Songwriter*. "Each song is different. There wasn't a set pattern I applied. I had to take each song as an individual and really listen to it. I go back to the architect analogy. It's like I was dealing with twelve different architects and some of their buildings and what components they used. I really had to find my way into each structure. It's a sonic structure, yes, but similar rules do apply." Tori's approach to the material was to keep the lyrics intact but re-envision the sound: "[M]usic is where you make your statement. And the statement is that you really don't change the words: you take a man's words and hand them right back to him. And it means something completely different without changing a word. That's what fascinated me." Though she was not writing original material, her talents as a songwriter were essential to her reimagining of the songs. Without that ability to reimagine from the "blueprints" of the songs, *Strange Little Girls* would not exist. Amos cleared permission to use the songs through the various record companies rather than directly approaching the artists themselves, not interested in seeking their approval.

The album's most provocative cover — Eminem's "'97 Bonnie and Clyde" — was Tori's way of giving voice to the woman murdered in the song's narrative. Said Amos, "I didn't change one word of the Eminem song. We gave him his say. And he wrote this. And now it's her turn, she is hearing, this is her vocal as she lay dying in the trunk. This is about showing that words can hurt and heal. It's about showing that you can take your power back as a woman or as a gay person. Clearly me and Eminem are on different sides politically, but bitching and moaning does not change anything. What changes things is when people become conscious and start questioning things for themselves." To examine a song from the opposite perspective to the original's was Amos's intent; with this track she gave voice to the wife forgotten: "Everyone's grooving to this tune, and nobody seemed to care about her."

Tori's version of "Strange Little Girl" had at its center "the little girl whose father killed her mother in Eminem's song, all grown up, having to deal with the fact that she was an accomplice to the murder. She's a dichotomy of things because she's divided — even when parents divorce, if they turn one child against one parent, you're dividing that child at the core." The original by The Stranglers positioned the girl as "very sexy" but with Amos singing the same lyrics it became a song about a girl in danger. For "I Don't Like Mondays," which was written about a 1979 school shooting in California, Amos took on the point of view of the female police officer who "goes to the school, finds the first body in the stairwell, then finds the girl who's killed everybody and kills her. [She] is licensed to do this; you would think that she's justified in her act, but she's having a difficult time with it because she doesn't think this particular girl is a bad seed." The ease with which a teenager was able to get a firearm was an issue in 1979 and sadly remained a problem 20 years later, which prompted Amos to layer in audio fragments of both Presidents Bush discussing the right to bear arms in "Happiness Is a Warm Gun." Of that song, Tori said, "It's been circling me for a few years now, because yes, we have a gun culture. And, yes, we have a Second Amendment. As you and I know, when it's easier to get a gun than a driver's license, something is just intrinsically wrong."

To represent the metalheads, *Strange Little Girls* features Slayer's "Raining Blood." Amos told *Spin*, "I was reading about what was going on in Afghanistan — the way women were being oppressed, the destruction of religious statues. And when I heard that song, I just imagined a huge juicy vagina coming out of the sky, raining blood over all those racist, misogynist fuckers." A longtime admirer of Neil Young, Amos saw something deeper going on in "Heart of Gold" as she deconstructed the lyrics. "When I stripped it back, I saw that there was a sort of fury in the song," said Amos. "I found this song to be this desperate cry for something." In "New Age," Tori saw a woman resolved to not sit out of the action any longer despite her fear of the titular new age; "Time" forced Amos to listen to what Death was saying; "Enjoy the Silence" spoke to her in the voice of a showgirl named Isis; and "Rattle-snakes" gave Tori a companion who she could have "really good chats" with over coffee. Amos saw "an androgynous being, like a seahorse" in "Real Men," while "I'm Not in Love" was channeled through Tori via "a little fetish girl — she's into BDSM." Choosing to end the record with "Real Men," Tori felt that song was the heart of the record with its "mantra of tolerance."

Once again happy to record in her studio in Cornwall away from the record company's prying eyes, Tori finished mapping out the album and prepared to begin recording: "Being in Cornwall is like living on location. About a month before we start recording a new album, the crew arrives and it's a very creative time as everyone just gets the feel of the area. It's not like we play hooky or go off fishing — well, the chef goes fishing, which is great — but it's more about osmosis, getting to know the land."

Marcel van Limbeek noted this album as a turning point in working out of Martian Studios: "The one thing about *Strange Little Girls*, and this is speaking for myself, but it wasn't [as much] a challenge as the previous records, because by now I felt comfortable in the studio. And for the first time, I had that feeling that all the decisions we'd made in the studio, they sort of translated outside the studio as well. What I mean is: when you're in the studio, you can make a judgment about a song — this is too boomy or too bright, or too dull or too wet or too dry — but if you're working in that studio for the first time, you don't know for sure if that's saying something about the studio or about the mix, if you know what I mean? And so the one thing I remember with *Strange Little Girls*, when the LP came out and I listened to those mixes in the car or at home, for the first time I thought, 'Well, we have it down with the studio now: whatever decisions we make in the studio, I can hear that it's working outside the studio as well.'"

Newcomer to the Tori Amos team for this album, legendary guitarist Adrian Belew told *Alternative Press* of the "real camaraderie" while recording: "The people around here give off a certain energy . . . It all works together. There was even a point when Tori was in the room dancing next to me while I was playing. That makes the whole thing have an electricity." Van Limbeek agreed, "Within our production team, what had changed from record to record up to that point is we'd gotten better and better, but with *Strange Little Girls*, our chemistry also with the band was at its best. With Matt [Chamberlain] and [bass player] Jon [Evans] too. Matt had come out for *Choirgirl Hotel* the first time around and was followed shortly afterward by Jon, and by the time of *Strange Little Girls*, they had become full members of the family, if you know what I mean. So that was not a big change, but we melded all in closer together." Once again acting as both performer and producer, Amos said, "Your job as a producer is to pull in a team that is right for a project. And all songs and concepts have bloodlines, whether they have been realized or not by another version . . . What's working is very apparent, and what's not is also very apparent." Said van Limbeek, "I think with that record, more than the previous ones, I think it would be fair to say she started looking at us to get input into what to do in shaping the covers. She would pick the songs, but in terms of what should go on them and what they should sound like, she definitely looked a bit more to Mark, and Matt and Jon, and perhaps myself, and we worked with Justin Meldal-Johnsen, he played bass for Beck; he came in for that record as well. He had some crazy, crazy bass sounds, so he definitely had an influence as well."

"We had really become a band," said Matt Chamberlain of the *Strange Little Girls* era. "The main thing that created that is Tori put trust in what we did as players. She's never told me what to play; she'll supply me with the story of what the song's about, or the mood she's trying to get, but she'll never tell me specifically what to do. I'll just try things and experiment and if she's into it, then she's into it, and usually it works. Most of the time, we'll go, 'Wow, that's pretty cool.' Luckily, we have the same aesthetic as far as what she wants for her songs, so I think that's the main reason why it feels like a band. I don't have to sit there trying to match her vision; it just kind of naturally happens. She just lets you do what you do as a player, and it just clicks, and she trusts you." Adrian Belew, guitarist for King Crimson and session player for, among others, David Bowie and Trent Reznor, was similarly encouraged by Amos, who told him to bring anything to the studio that's "currently intriguing": "I had just recently acquired a fretless guitar synthesizer. There may be only one in the world. It's a fretless guitar, and it also operates as a synthesizer. So I played it on the Neil Young song. . . . The ending of 'Happiness Is a Warm Gun' turned into a blues version, and it was inspiring enough to me that I discovered a different way of playing guitar. I turned my tremolo device in a different way — I'd never seen anyone do that — and it caused me to play in a unique way."

Accompanying Amos, as always, was her trusty Bösendorfer, of which — or whom — Tori said, "She is an entity in itself. She has got a difficult character. Pianos are grand. They are as wise as the ocean. To understand her, you have got to speak her language. She can be very exacting. She does not tolerate everybody." Tori also used the Fender Rhodes on her version of Tom Waits' "Time" and on "Rattlesnakes" where she created a back-and-forth delay to invoke the movement of a snake's tail. A rare Amos track where she opted to take the keys out was "I'm Not in Love"; Tori explained that she wanted the song "to be almost like an ancient Japanese dance, like a ritual dance. So I stripped the keyboards off, and it became all about the vocal."

Chamberlain remembers that by *Strange Little Girls*, "Tori wasn't working with Andy Gray anymore, the programmer, and I thought, 'Man, I better step it up and get a little bit more into this.' So I went out and bought an Akai MPC2500 drum machine, and it was a new and exciting way for me to work with her. Every record's been different, we

Matt Chamberlain at the drums, playing at Radio City Music Hall in New York City while on tour with Tori Amos in 2009.

mix it up every time we get together. So on that record, I said, 'Hey, I'm going to bring out this Akai MPC with some modular synth filtering pedals, and run my drums through that and make beats.' And she'll say, 'Yeah, that sounds great, bring it out.' There were a lot of songs on that album that had programming, but Tori is also someone who likes real drums, and so do I. So wherever we could get programming in, we'd do it, but for most of the album, I played live drums.

"For that record, I brought out a couple old British kits, and that was the first record where we set the drums up in the studio's main room, and it just sounded so great. Also, prior to that, I had been working with Jon Bryon, producer on the Fiona Apple record, her second, where we'd discovered that if you stick a microphone — a full fidelity, really nice mic, for instance a U 47 or C 12 — right by the drummer's ear, pointing down toward the snare and kick drum, it takes a general picture of the whole kit and its drummer's perspective. So that when you're playing the drums, and making them sound good to your ears, then if you stick a mic by your ears, it's just going to sound great. So on that record we ended up using a c 12 for the drummer's perspective mic. Also, I remember as well as bringing out electronic stuff, I would bring out a lot of percussion — like some oil drums I'd had a friend weld springs to, and other special percussion instruments that had grown out of my exploring more of how to make a drum kit out of different percussion instruments. That's always been part of my rig live, where I bring a drum kit, some electronic stuff, and then the percussion so we can kind of go to any of those worlds we need to, because with Tori, you never what's going to happen — either live or in the studio."

The project took a lot out of Tori — by the time they were mixing, she said, "My head hurt" — but the album struck a provocative musical chord, one that Atlantic Records general manager Ron Shapiro reasoned should be expected. To the *Los Angeles Times*, he said, "When you do songs that are beloved by many people you almost always strike a nerve, and hopefully it will be positive and enlightening. . . . But Tori's always been brave enough not to be afraid of extreme reactions. In fact, she provokes them and God bless her for doing so." The album marked the end of Tori Amos's time with Atlantic, her seemingly endless contract now fulfilled. Critics were in agreement that Amos's new LP was, as *Rolling Stone* put it, "dangerous work" and it landed on *Spin*'s 2001 Albums of the Year list at #10. *Strange Little Girls*, released in September 2001, featured an impressive album package, with Tori dressed up in the character of each song and accompanied by text describing each "strange little girl" written by her dear friend and bestselling novelist Neil Gaiman.

The time spent inhabiting the songs on *Strange Little Girls* affected Tori as a songwriter: "I have discovered these women but I don't control them. I'm really curious myself if they will resurface on my next records." Always writing, always burning with creative energy, it was not long before Amos's curiosity, and her fans', was satisfied with her next studio album.

"It's as much an inner trip, with all the extraordinary people that [Scarlet] meets, as a real walk across a wounded and disoriented country. We all have questions with no answers, our fears, our joys, our desires, our beliefs, and the ones we lost."

— TORI AMOS (*KEYBOARD*, 2003)

CHAPTER 9

Scarlet's Walk
(2002)

Strange Little Girls marked the end of an era for Amos — her last album with Atlantic. Explained Amos, "I asked to get off Atlantic years and years ago. It was a bad relationship, a bad marriage. And they wouldn't be gracious and let me go. So I maneuvered my way and found people that were of like mind [at Epic]." Tori Amos's eighth studio album also marked a change in her writing process; the songs came to her in segments and snatches over years, beginning back when she was pregnant with Natashya. She stored away the eight or 16 bars that came to her, until the time was right to work on an entire album's worth of original material. In a 2002 interview with *Hot Press*, Amos said, "I usually find the melody first, but often married to a word or phrase in such a way that you can't separate them. And these words and melodies are like cornerstones that you work around. You know when it's right because you can feel it, like touching something hot. And I didn't know what relationship these ideas had to each other, these pieces of songs. I thought, 'I don't know what this is yet.' And then I found myself in New York City on September 11 and I felt an opening, or a question."

In New York to promote *Strange Little Girls*, Amos found herself in the midst of a tragedy. "Being in the group, in the place where that's happening," related Amos to *Music Monthly*, "you can smell that burning, that smell of wounding, of many people and a being and a land and an ideology . . . in deep pain. Everywhere you turn it's almost like you're walking through the center of her wound. I was in and out of the city a lot. I wanted to see my baby, who was down in Florida, but at the same time you didn't want to leave New York. It was almost as if you needed to keep a vigil for her, if you could. If you hadn't lost somebody personally, you needed to be there to hold a space, to light a candle, to bring the bandages — not the physical bandages, the emotional bandages." Deciding not to cancel her tour in response to fan emails requesting that she stay on the road and provide a place for people to get together, Amos found the germ of the album born in the wake of destruction and tragedy. Said Amos in 2003, "I had no idea when I started what I wanted the work to be, but as I got more and more drawn into it, I began to see that America was a character and that she was being personified by the women. That's how I was getting to know the soul of this country, by meeting these women." Searching for the "soul of what America is," the idea of a journey or road trip began to shape the spirit of the songs that would become *Scarlet's Walk*. To vh1, Amos revealed, "[My grandfather] related to America as a spirit. He would talk about her like she was a sister and a friend. So I've seen her like that since I was little. But as I got older, I started associating America with her politics. When the twins went down, that brought me back. I felt the loss of somebody I cared about."

"On the road, it was a time when people were telling us stories — in letters, before and after shows," Amos said in an interview with *USA Today*. "I've never experienced an openness like that, where people needed so much to talk, because nobody knew what tomorrow would bring — or if there would be a tomorrow. People in different cities responded in different ways, but for once we weren't isolated. After thirty or forty years of living in a grown-up Disneyland, where we felt no one could hurt us, we were finally experiencing what it's like to be part of the world." Amos called the album a "sonic novel" in which she

took on the character of Scarlet, making her way across the country and meeting "people from all different cultures and walks of life — Native Americans, right-wing truck drivers, cowboys, porn stars, librarians." She listens, questions, and reflects; said Amos of the album, "There's a lot of beauty and love, and there's sorrow there, too. It is about loss, but it's also about stories and characters, and people that my character runs into."
The notion of America as a nation merged with the individual and the idea of place: "When you talk about somebody's body map — an idea that I've been circling for awhile — I think that we all have an invisible map. And at a certain point in your life, you can begin to look and really see which places resonate with you, pull you in. You might have only been to a place one time; you might not have even been there at all, but it's a place that gives you a physical response. And that's something that I was going for with *Scarlet's Walk*. I wanted *Scarlet's Walk* to be a space for people to come and network and trade ideas."

For Amos, the songs on the album comprised a history of America, capturing the soul and voice of the country in a tumultuous time: "There started to become a response to the government saying, 'If you question the government, then you're unpatriotic.' It hurt people at first, and then it started to offend some people — how the tragedy was getting manipulated, and it's still being manipulated. So Scarlet was driven to ask questions about what she believed in." Noting how her music had progressed from the personal to the political over the course of her career, Amos said, "I think this record has been humbling. *Little Earthquakes* was very much about my character in crisis, and that's not really what *Scarlet's Walk* is about. It's about different people at different times in crisis."

Each song was born of a particular narrative thread; said Amos, "I'm the librarian. The songs work as individual short stories. But this is a narrative and if you want to look at it like that, it works on that

level, too. I wrote a work that if you want to take it as far as you can, the blueprints and architecture are there." Continually evolving as an artist, Amos could see that her songwriting was changing as she crafted *Scarlet's Walk*. Comparing her current work to previous albums, Amos felt "*Scarlet's Walk* is very structured in a classic songwriting style. I guess as a songwriter, you go through different phases. I think there's an organic approach to this record. *Boys for Pele* also had an organic approach, but the songwriting style was much different, because it was more improvisational. There was a more modern approach on [*From the Choirgirl Hotel* and *To Venus and Back*], as far as songwriting and, more than anything, sound. So those records reflected the time and what I was experimenting with." For *Scarlet's Walk*, Amos studied great albums from the 1970s: "It's patterned more after classic song structure — Fleetwood Mac's *Rumours*, Neil Young's *Harvest*. I think that I was trying to just immerse myself in the way things were recorded. It was a real craftsmanship. . . . It's very hand done. Handmade. And so we approached it like that." As the album took the shape of a "road trip," Amos wanted to capture that nostalgic quality.

Perhaps even more critical for Amos was capturing the sound of the land — the distinct places and cultures in America reflected in Scarlet's walk through the nation. To *Women Who Rock*, she explained, "I think that the songs were similar to song lines in aboriginal culture. They were my key to take me to places. It's almost as if I were following a crossword puzzle and clues within the songs themselves. And so work started when I began seeing imagery come in; we start going back to threads, because, after all, 'scarlet' is a thread. And I was following the etymology of the word." A thread before it was a color, Amos connected to the symbolism of the word "scarlet," "weaving and pulling on Native American history, their past and their spiritual walk." She put together a research team from Haskell Indian Nations University in Lawrence, Kansas, with the help of Manny King, a friend and the registrar of the college.

On the broad theme of the album, Tori explained, "America is a character in this story. She shapeshifts, using that Native American belief . . . So she's personified in Amber Waves and carved in the manic-depressive woman, and the old Apache woman by the fire, and on and on. Besides Scarlet, the women are where you find slices of that cherry pie. The men, of course, are terra firma — earth. I like that idea." The opening track of the album, "Amber Waves," drew its name from a character in P.T. Anderson's *Boogie Nights*, the porn actress played by Julianne Moore. "You find so many stories in Los Angeles," said Amos. "You see especially where all the movies come from — and how the game of chess works. Amber Waves is part of it — if she represents America or if she's a woman, everybody decides for his- or herself. There's this anthem ["America the Beautiful"] with [the lyric] 'amber waves of grain' in it — and then there is this porn star in *Boogie Nights*. She notices at a certain point that she has to learn to appreciate herself. L.A. doesn't appreciate unconventional personalities." In an interview with MTV, Tori explained how "Amber Waves" was the right place to begin the journey of *Scarlet's Walk*: "She's lost pieces of herself that she can't seem to reclaim. So the story takes off from there, and I meet people along the way. Events happen that make me question what I believe in and make me question what my country has been up to, and I start searching out answers: who are the good guys? Because it doesn't seem like the ones that are calling themselves the good guys are doing the things I thought they were in the country's name." The character of Amber Waves, from Tori Amos's perspective, was a fitting pronouncement on the state of the union: "This porn-star woman looks around after years of her life and realizes that she can't get back the pieces of herself she's sacrificed to become who she is. There's a line in that song that says, 'There's not a lot of me left anymore . . .' I think, as a nation, America might be in a similar position."

From there the album moved into a song that captured the nostalgia of a road trip quite literally, as a couple travels through California on Highway 101 in "A Sort of Fairytale": "'Fairytale' is where I go off with the person I believe to be the love of my life. But we split up. The love of your life should work, shouldn't it? The story is a sort of fairytale — why don't they stay together?" In "Wednesday," the broken love story continues as the heroine is "in a place now where she realizes that love is a bit complicated because it's not a cut and dried sort of idea. . . . I think you might be really very taken with somebody and they might be very much in your life but there are things that they do that are quite disrespectful or cross a line in a way that is very passive-aggressive so you can't really talk about it. Manipulation makes her cry, especially with people you're supposed to be close with."

Personal struggles encompass the ideas of war and violence so top of mind to the country's situation in songs like "Sweet Sangria" — "She believes in his cause but can't load the gun. She doesn't believe in death of innocents" — and "Pancake," which Amos described as "about the abuse of power, whether by presidents or rock stars. There seems to be a right wing ideology held by some young hipsters — Jesse Helms in tattoos. This thinking has to find something to hate, whether it's a gay person, a woman, a different race or a different religion." The tragedy that had first inspired *Scarlet's Walk* is honored in "I Can't See New York," a song that "flashed in my mind as soon as disaster struck New York on September 11." In the lyrics, Amos explores the idea that "we see the culmination of outer betrayal that may have stemmed from some kind of inner betrayal."

Drawn from a more personal place was "Taxi Ride" dedicated to Kevyn Aucoin, the legendary makeup artist and photographer who died in 2002. Said Tori, "The odd thing about 'Taxi Ride' was that this song was being written before he died, and he even heard that line, 'just another dead fag to you.' . . . Kevyn and I were having conversations, and I didn't know what was coming. But I knew he was in a lot of pain, and he felt betrayed by people who weren't there when he was in need. Then everybody who shows up in his death can give a statement, but they weren't there in the trenches. His death brought up a lot of things in people — some lovely and some despicable and disgusting. 'Taxi' is for Kevyn."

Motherhood was an important theme for Amos as she wrote the album: drawing from the innate protectiveness she felt for her daughter growing up in such a troubled world as well as the idea of the mother in nationhood. Said Amos, "The whole journey is that [Scarlet] becomes a physical mother and realizes, in the end, that to mother her daughter, to leave her anything, she has to mother her spiritual mother, which is

America." As particular as Amos's inspirations were as she wrote *Scarlet's Walk*, she knew that in the end, any listener would have his or her own unique relationship to her creation: "People have to have their own experience with the music. Once you put it out there, it's between them and the songs."

Once the album was written and it was nearing time to record at Martian Engineering, Tori Amos had to prepare for her other role — producer. In addition to the usual team, new musicians were recruited, notably guitarists Robbie McIntosh and David Tom. Said Amos of producing, "I think that it's very difficult being the artist and the producer, 'cause you have to change hats. The artist sometimes just can't head certain conversations, but these conversations have to take place. It has taken me quite a few years to learn to be a good captain. When I'm not captain, then I'm the ship. And that's what the artist is, the artist is the ship — and you just hope she's not the *Titanic*! And you also hope that the captain can hear you say, 'We're running into an iceberg!'" Once again she was working alongside her husband, Mark Hawley. "I always feel like I'm in a new adventure with him," said Amos. "It's delicious to work with someone who constantly makes you surpass yourself and with whom you have a passionate relationship. For nothing in the world would I change this way of working."

The Native American influence that had helped shape the lyrics was also something Amos wanted reflected in the sound. In an interview with the *Baltimore Sun*, she explained, "I wanted to capture a natural light from the sun and shadow. I wanted to achieve that sonically. I wanted to go after what comes from the organic, natural world. Once I knew the elements — this woman getting to know the soul of America — I had a research team to pull everything together to make it airtight. It's probably the most time I've spent writing and researching a record."

The process, as she explained to *Music Monitor*, involved sourcing sounds and instrumentation native to locales that connected to each song: "I got the musicians and engineers together, and showed them on the map where I felt the songs were aligned with, the references in the songs themselves. . . . 'Well, this happens here, and what are the cultures that settled here?' We know the Native American culture that was around here, so we had a little reference team looking up the skins, the drumming, what was going on."

Central to that regional idea was the percussion. "The drums sort of represented the soul of the land, and Matt and I worked very closely about the cultures that were in each particular geographic setup," said Amos. "So we would look and, for instance, in Texas, you have a huge Latino, even Cuban influence, so we want to bring in the low rider, sinister, he's a Mexican Revolutionary, the guy in 'Sweet Sangria.' And how do we translate that into sound? 'Don't Make Me Come to Vegas' is sort of a Cuban lounge, with blazing saddles and a high heel. So we were trying to go to the land for the clues."

Drummer Matt Chamberlain explained his view on the album and how it marked a shift in Amos's career and his approach to playing: "*Strange Little Girls* was the last album Tori was contractually obligated to Atlantic Records for, and so her next record, *Scarlet's Walk*, marked kind of a new era for her — new label — and she wanted to do this more Americana-based record, where she wanted to abandon all electronics and be a little bit more heartfelt, acoustic, and organic, and just see what would happen as a band if we were put in that position. The whole story of the record was about this little character named Scarlet that travels all over America, and so it made sense that Tori wanted to be more musically like America. On *Scarlet's Walk*, I thought 'Well, if we're going to go acoustic . . .' I brought out these gigantic John Bonham–sized drums, a twenty-six-inch bass drum, and some of it was a Ludwig [Crystalite] drum kit, which is a see-through Plexiglas drum kit, just like the one Bonham used in 'The Song Remains the Same.' It was funny to think about because that record, *Scarlet's Walk*, was really warm sounding, even though we were using plastic drums on a couple of the songs, just as a juxtaposition to her real sweet, acoustic piano. I thought that would be a great thing to have: these real aggro drums going off over her playing really beautiful piano. For the rest of the record, we changed quite a bit between an old Rodgers kit from the sixties, and there are a couple of songs on the record where the drums are very muffled, seventies sounding. For those tracks, we'd moved the drums into this really dead room where there was no reflection on the walls. It was all phonics on the walls, like foam, sound-recording material like they'd have in the seventies.

"For that record, mic-wise, the Sony c-37a had definitely become our stationary snare drum mic, and there were two c 12s put up in this miking pattern that I had first learned from Ethan Johns, son of legendary record producer Glyn Johns. The miking pattern for a lot of those Stones and Zeppelin records Glyn had produced was you stick a mic above the drum kit, above the snare drum, so it would act as an overhead mic — one mono overhead. And then a mic in the drummer's perspective position by the ear, or maybe even lower, just kind of off to the right. Then a bass drum mic. The trick with this was with the two overhead mics, you had to get the distance from the middle of the snare drum equally distant for phasing — so you had the drummer's perspective mic and the top overhead mics equally distant with the bass drum mic. So the trio of mics had to be in the right distance from each other for the phase to work properly, and it does sound good. So most of that record was recorded with that setup."

Engineer Marcel van Limbeek recalled, "On that album, we'd found a whole new room that we started tracking drums in at the studio. On all the prior albums, the drums had been recorded in the second-biggest recording room, since the biggest one is where Tori keeps her piano and where we'd record strings. So for *Scarlet's Walk*, we moved the drums to another room which was a much more live room, and it connected up to yet another room that we made completely dense. You can open the door between them, and then vary the amount of ambience you have on your instrument by moving it deeper into the dead room or more to the live room. So we started recording drums in there, and using c 12s as overhead mics. That was a big change because it added nice top end on the drum kit." As for Tori's piano and vocal parts, they were recorded in a manner that harkened back to the recording setup of *Choirgirl*: "We basically took the box model from the church and replaced it with a big screen. So we had that same idea, but we replaced it with screens, and we built a big, wooden screen with acoustic foam on top, that goes over the keyboard of the piano and stops any direct sound of the vocal coming into the piano mics, and any direct piano sound coming back into the vocal mics. Vocally, on *Scarlet's Walk*, we switched between an AKG C 12 mic at the time and a Neumann U 67 mic, and we also used that Sony mic here and there, but mainly the C 12 and U 67."

Recording an artist who sings and plays at the same time makes crosstalk an issue, something that Hawley and van Limbeek were used to dealing with by the time they recorded *Scarlet's Walk*. Said van Limbeek: "With Tori, you get her hitting pedals while she plays on the vocal mic, but that's fine. With her music, a certain amount of crosstalk you always get, and in a way it helps, it makes her sound richer. So when she hits the pedal loud, you will hear it. It's part of her music, part of her performance." For an album like *Scarlet's Walk* that emphasized a band sound, it's "obviously a more complicated process," said van Limbeek, "and typically [the way] we dive into it is that we will already have finalized the vocal sound. And, even though we track the vocal just microphone, pre-amp, then straight onto the hard drive, during the recording process, we will have worked out EQ settings, which we'll write down, and will have come up with vocal effects we store, and so we really will have finalized the vocal sound. Then we mix everything else around it. When Tori plays piano by itself, then the Bösendorfer is the whole band, but if you have the full band with Matt and Jon and the piano and a bunch of guitars, that's a big challenge. That's something that came together really well on *Scarlet's Walk*, where it had always been a challenge of mixing that big piano and all the other instruments and making it sound good — that came together on that album."

Proud of the results from the studio, van Limbeek said, "*Scarlet's Walk* sounds so good because it's them playing live. The majority of all the songs you listen to are full takes of piano, drums, bass, and vocals. They rehearsed for a long time, then put it down, and me and Mark captured it. So *Scarlet's Walk* came together in terms of the way it sounds; it really reinforced Tori's songwriting — it was a really great record."

Fans were hungry for a new album of originals from Tori, resulting in 583,000 copies of *Scarlet's Walk* sold in its first week and a debut at #7 on the Billboard Top 200 Album chart. *CMJ* magazine's review of the record captured fans' sentiments about the artist and her music: "*Scarlet's Walk* stands as a testimony both to Tori Amos's staying power and her continued ability to enrapture listeners while remaining wholeheartedly unique." Amos herself felt a sense of accomplishment with this album that she didn't always feel: "I think there are a couple [albums] that I've done that are complete works. And *Scarlet's Walk* is one that seems to be a complete work."

"I have to admit that a honeybee like me likes a good buzz."

— TORI AMOS (*WINDY CITY TIMES*, 2005)

CHAPTER 10

The Beekeeper (2005)

Like *Scarlet's Walk* and America, Tori Amos's next studio album was very much shaped by a place: in this case, her home in Cornwall, England. Writing there, on the shores of the Atlantic, shaped her compositions. The concept of "the beekeeper," said Amos, sprang from the tradition "within the Celts and the Welsh that has sustained all the invasions that this little island has had to take on board and I think that it spoke to me." Its endurance inspired her, as she explained to *Paste*: "[W]hatever civilization is going on, right wing or left wing, the bees have got to pollinate. And this tradition has sustained through different religious wars and ideologies, which really affected me because it's so intertwined with nature."

Once again researching her concept with the dedication of a scholar, Amos turned to Simon Buxton's *The Shamanic Way of the Bee* (2004), which "began to verify some of the research that I had been gathering. The bee masters and bee mistresses were very much alive in Eastern Europe; very much like Tolkien and the cultures he was writing about. The beekeepers were the parallels to our Native American shamans. I wanted to find the ancient cultures before the current religions had taken their tolls; so I went back to the culture of bees." Buxton's book explored "the balance between nature itself, and that the bees were holding this sacred space of sexuality, procreation that goes on in the garden. Reading the bee master's account, I began to see the beekeeper as this creative force, this neutral force in our story." Amos connected that idea to her role as a songwriter: "great composers are collectors of ideas first . . . They are able to unite different ideas that might not work on their own but together are complete, a pollination of ideas."

Another idea Amos captured in the beekeeper theme was that of the hexagon. "The concept is that there are six gardens, no different than that there are six sides to the cell in the beehive, so the hexagon shape is sort of our kind of key," said Amos, with each garden representing a part of the female character embodied in the album as a whole. "Biblical mythology and the ancient feminine mysteries are joined together," she told ThePop.de. "As I began to realize that the gardens personified the different relationships a woman could have, the songs started coming and coming." Exploring mythic archetypes from Egyptian warrior goddess Sekhmet to Buddhist goddess Kuan-Yin, from the Norse tradition's Freya to Irish Queen Maeve, *The Beekeeper* also responded to modern ideas of Christianity. In particular, as Amos explained to *Spin*, "The idea for *Beekeeper* came after listening to politicians talk about the Bible and thinking about something so old being very current because people are still arguing about it. As a minister's daughter, I felt it was time that I go into the teachings that I was brought up with and maybe turn them around a bit." Across religious texts, Amos felt, "There are strong forces in the society that have kidnapped our holy writings. These forces drive some kind of emotional blackmailing. I was particularly occupied with the thought of how the church's men have edited the teaching of Jesus to their advantage and at the cost of women. What if we all have been manipulated?" In *The Beekeeper*, Amos wanted to reexamine those texts.

The woman — who stands in for all women — in *The Beekeeper* eats from the tree of knowledge in the garden of life, and then "experiences all kinds of emotions from passion to betrayal, to selfless love, to temptation, to seduction, to disappointment and bereavement.

The songs capture different stages of her journey and explore her different feelings." A journey "from passion to enlightenment," *The Beekeeper* examined Amos's notions of the feminine and the divine and, she said, "The whole crux of this work is to marry the sexual and the sacred, which has been circumcised from women in the Christian church." In an interview with *Rag*, Amos revealed, "[I]f there is one thing that I have gotten in my letters over the years

— this is what I read the most — which is the division of women from their sexual self and their spiritual self. And in the religions, they do not talk about women unifying these into wholeness and that sexuality can become sacred. You're either the mistress or you're the mother. You can't be the mother and the hot mistress all within the same Being — if you look at these different archetypes. And it's essential that women feel that they can do this. I really felt like it was essential at this time — that there was a union of sexuality and sacredness within the theme."

On the flip side of that idea of the feminine, and still central to *The Beekeeper*'s concept, is "the abuse of power by the patriarchy of our leaders. See, the bee colony is based on a female hierarchy. The honeybee gathers the honey and feeds the hive . . . I felt that it was essentially something to address the abuse of the male hierarchy in our current world. I'm talking ideology more than anything, not just about men and women." As with *Scarlet's Walk*, Amos felt this album "chronicles not just my personal life but also our time, whereas some of the earlier records were more about me. I'm looking at what's occurring with the mass consciousness."

Speaking more broadly about how she generates her songs, Amos told *Uncut*, "I write from what I observe and as a result, all my songs are an expression of what I've experienced or thought or witnessed. Sometimes I write from my own perspective and sometimes I'm hidden in the songs so you might not know I'm even there. In real

life I might have been the one that wasn't so kind, but I'm singing it from the other person's perspective because it makes it a stronger story." Amos explained her purpose in writing — what she hopes to create for the listener — in an interview with the *Virginian Post*: "If you're able to allow yourself to walk in this world, then you can begin to understand the language. It's no different than when you're talking with a computer. I make mazes for you to walk into that are filled with light filament. Sometimes it's about where you are. Sometimes you have to look at the part of yourself that's a terrorist. It's very easy to spot the stranger carrying a bomb in a knapsack. What's very tricky is within our own personal universes, where we don't know how to tell a friend they've overstayed their welcome, or when they've not treated you fairly. That's where we're tested. That's what I write about."

Of her process, Amos revealed that she's still using an old tape recorder to capture songs as they come to her: "Mark and Marcel hopelessly want me to put on a digital one. It's like a catalog, I record everything, day after day. And I examine it regularly." Some ideas are put away for years before they are brought out again to be made complete. When the compulsion to compose strikes Tori, she says, "you can pick up from this catalog and finally have sonic shapes, made of all these components that you can link between them. When I do this musical collecting, I also see images, words that go along with it. Then the lyrics come, after the music, just like if they were alive. Then I play regularly the results to Mark and Marcel so that they can have an idea of the direction that I'm taking."

While composing, Amos feels more like she's divining than hatching ideas out of nowhere: "There has always been a relationship with the sonic world and that is that I've always believed that it exists. I'm not the only creator. I co-create with this — call it 'the muse,' call it just 'creativity itself.' And I have to always continually increase my musical vocabulary and the lyric side of things and I look at a lot of visual arts and start collecting these treasures and these ideas I have and I put them in this ever-rotating palette . . . So instead of paints I have words and musical patterns that I collect, and this becomes my musical canvas." Her desire to research, to experience other forms of art and creative expression, fuels her own creativity. To be a songwriter, says Amos, "You've got to expand your ideas. It's about stretching yourself. Sometimes I just open a dictionary at random, just look at where it falls open, pick a word and start from there." On this album, Amos was attempting to achieve "an effect . . . that would embody what a honeybee does when she goes to the organ of a flower and gets the nectar . . . and delicately spreads it around. She creates this prolific work, just by being a honeybee."

The album's title track was partly inspired by the sudden death of her brother, Michael, in a car accident. "The song 'The Beekeeper' was in process when he had his tragic accident. I didn't have the background vocals done yet and I was able to weave into 'The Beekeeper' the sorrow and the loss of Michael on the song, as well as the infinity dance of the honeybee. The honeybee represents sacred sexuality and represents transmutation from one plane to the next. The subject matters — including Michael's death — were really transformational." Of "The Power of Orange Knickers," Tori explained, "Well, I wanted to write a song about terrorists. It's a word that's been used and misused a lot in the last few years. Therefore, sometimes to emancipate a word, you have to undress it. And as I started to undress it, I found a lot of things there. And if you start exploring it, all the correlations and just the word associations, you might get certain images in your mind." In writing the lyrics, Amos "put the word 'kiss' in there to create a paradox as it's the furthest thing from 'terrorist.' I've always been a John Lennon person. My husband is a Paul McCartney person but I love a twist in the story. I love the tension of opposites. I love dancing with the devil — but the devil's a dictionary, not a dick." Ultimately, the song's message is that "using the idea of terrorism to get what you want — whoever you are — should be a thing of the past." "Original Sinsuality," the singer explained, retells the story of Genesis, but in Amos's garden, it is not a sin to eat from the Tree of Knowledge. In "Mother Revolution," Amos explored "a consciousness": "It's the mothers refusing to get drawn into the guilt — from the time of Troy and the ancients to our current circumstances — of not wanting their son or daughter's blood spilled for an agenda." A painting by Seurat, *Seated Woman with a Parasol*, inspired Amos to write "Parasol": "I was drawn to it and I started to think about Victorian women and then some women today, the type of women who don't want to intimidate their partner and so allow themselves to become reduced so the other person can feel confident." Daphne du Maurier's novel *Jamaica Inn* lent its title to Amos's song about a man and a woman falling apart.

In terms of the sound of the album, said Amos, "I didn't want to mirror [the destruction around us] with discordant music. In making raw honey, there needed to be a smoothness and harmonic agreement between nature and creature . . . What I wanted to create, with organ and piano, joining flower and bee, was not conflict but procreation, in a time where procreation can be deemed as sinful." A central feature of the record's overall sonic composition was Amos marrying the piano and the B3 Hammond organ for the first time. The organ, a Christmas present from her husband, "has a very different sound to other organs and I liked the idea of using it alongside the Bösendorfer piano because I wanted the music to represent the pollination that goes on in the garden. To me, the Hammond is a very funky, masculine instrument whilst the piano is more emotive and feminine. On *The Beekeeper*, they come together to form a perfect union."

Despite her newfound affection for the B3 Hammond, Amos still felt the connection to her first instrument. To *Keyboard*, she related her deep connection to the piano, "Every piano — the notes, the sound of the relationships is unique . . . If I played this on my Bösendorfer, it would be ever so slightly different. And if your ears are open to that, if you're not too deaf from listening to music through the years, it triggers the next answer. You begin to pioneer again every time you're able to really listen to an instrument. Without leaving the room, I feel like I travel into the universe of sound . . . I've been able to have a confidence in the spirit of the creature we call the piano . . . Over the years, in situations where I have invested time and energy and become disappointed in the outcomes — in projects, in people, in creativity itself — the piano has never let me down. The piano has never bailed. The essence itself has always been there to allow me to take chances and to push me in a way."

Unlike her connection to her instrument, which began in early childhood, Amos's relationship with her bandmates was something relatively new and that grew and developed on each album and each tour. "When you're with the guys as not just the singer, but the player and composer," explained Amos to *Live Daily*, "something very . . . I have to be careful about my words, but you form a marriage with each man. It's not sexual. Therefore, I was able to form a bond with Matt and Jon, a threesome, like ZZ Top without the beards. . . . For the tour for *Scarlet's Walk*, when I toured with them, I think we formed a language that was captured on *The Beekeeper*, because that record is very much about keys and rhythm — the marriage between the bass and drums, and a piano player, in a classic jazz-combo style without the jazz. That's what I wanted. I wanted the joining of the male and the female, and I think — because we played over one hundred and fifty shows on *Scarlet's Walk* together as a threesome — I was able to go write music around them. I designed these songs for the male as well as the female, not just the girl alone at her piano."

Matt Chamberlain's perspective on Tori's musical frame of mind heading into recording was that "for *The Beekeeper*, I think after doing all the records we'd done where the studio was like a mad-scientist laboratory out in Cornwall, I think she wanted to get really simple and just play on that record. That was the mindset, like, 'Hey, why do we need to kill ourselves, how about you just play drums, I'll play piano, Jon will play bass, and we'll just record.' Jon is a great, great bassist, and he can decipher her insane way of voicing chords, and her harmonic structures and stuff, where I'm not sure she always knows how to describe it, and Jon is one of those musicians who has a good ear and can hear a chord, and say, 'That's a C sharp, flat 5.' So once he deciphers what's going on, he can figure out musically what to play around it. He and I grew up listening to the same kind of music, and our vocabulary as a rhythm section is such that when we're playing together, we're drawing from a lot of that. So a lot of times we'll look at each other and start laughing, because we're drawing from the same influences — stuff like the obvious Led Zeppelin and great American songwriters that everyone grew up listening to, like The Beatles, then there's the jazz world, which we're both deeply in. All the Miles Davis stuff and the later sixties experimental stuff Coltrain was into. So that record was the first record with Tori where I felt like she was going with a real pop sound deliberately, and the songs were very, very pop. "

Describing the atmosphere during recording sessions for *The Beekeeper*, Marcel van Limbeek revealed, "Tori was in a good and happy space on that record — early on through the time of *Choirgirl*, she'd gone through quite a few personal problems. She'd suffered a couple miscarriages, and things hadn't gone too well in that way for Mark and Tori, so by the time of *Beekeeper*, they'd had a beautiful daughter, who was healthy and doing really well. Tori had all her friends in her beautiful studio, so I don't know if that record directly is about that atmosphere, but it definitely comes across in the performances.

"Tori never really was a night owl. When we started working with her, I remember her telling us that she had a really good voice early in the morning. Then soon enough, she found out that Mark and I are simply too grumpy to be working with her in the morning, so typically she will work quite a bit in the morning, then we record all the way through the afternoon till dinnertime, but not usually after dinner. After dinner, what we might do is listen to some other music, or the record itself and come up with ideas, but usually there is no more recording. The baby being born did change Mark and Tori's recording process in terms of scheduling definitely. Before that, we would work twenty-four hours a day, depending on what the mood was like, and if we felt like recording at two in the morning, we'd do so. It's a bit less rock and roll nowadays — except when the band is playing, of course."

With Jon playing bass in the control room with Marcel and Mark, while Matt played drums in a room close to Amos's piano room at Martian Engineering, Amos laid down the base of some of the tracks for *Beekeeper* with the B3 Hammond first. Explained Amos to *Recording Musician*, "When that was the case, we would only record Matt and me together. Generally the song is just a skeleton for Matt that he completes after. . . . Then Mark and Marcel put together the piano and drums on Pro Tools. Then Matt is going to build a groove and Jon is going to re-think everything. . . . But first is what I play, my performance, and they play on what already exists."

As he had on *Scarlet's Walk*, Chamberlain brought out his "John Bonham drums" for the more pop-sounding tracks. Said the drummer, "If she's going to write these really beautiful songs, it'd be great to hear these bombastic drums behind them. So I brought some of that out, and I also brought out a couple smaller kits, hip-hop sounding where the snare is really high-pitched and tiny and a shorter, smaller kick drum with a shorter tone. For this record, I also had my laptop going so I could make drum loops from what we were doing live. I was thinking, 'Man, this could be a cool record to do some super-pop and hip-hop rhythms as far as the drums go,' but in her kind of way, which isn't necessarily true to the traditions of anything, it's more a hybrid. I also brought out a cocktail drum kit, which is a sixties kit where you stand and play, and used that on a couple songs. A lot of that album was a process of experimenting and trying to see what kind of kits worked best against these really poppy songs, and in other cases, she just wanted straight-up drum kits, nothing special."

Amos wanted the feeling of bees, the swarm and the rhythm, captured in the album. Explained Amos to *Music Monthly*, "[Y]ou're getting a complex rhythm, no different than you would in a swarm of bees . . . Their wings beat differently. So that's what we were working off of, that within the hive itself the structure is complex, yet it's very structured. So there's just this paradox that we wanted to work off of. So yes, the rehearsal time for the musicians was longer. The musicians had to put in more time on this, and I think you feel it because people sound more relaxed."

Though *The Beekeeper* landed at #5 on the Billboard Top 200 Album chart after its release in February 2005, Amos had a healthy attitude about those sorts of accomplishments: "If you want to be a popular artist with every record in the charts then you need to be honest about that and make your records accordingly. You can't get angry if ten years later you feel like you've sold out and disrespected your talent. Personally, I can take or leave success. The most important thing for me as a composer, is that each piece of work I create is one I'm proud of." And the critics responded to *The Beekeeper*: the *New York Times* called it her "most down-to-earth album in years."

"Music is a mirror that lets the listener say, 'I can be in the stillness in this two-bar phrase, so I can be in the stillness in my life.' And that might not seem like a lot, but this is how you expand the soul."

— TORI AMOS (*PERFORMING SONGWRITER*, 2006)

CHAPTER 11

American Doll Posse
(2007)

"When the songs started coming to me this time, I was looking for the continuity from song to song and I wasn't finding it. Not at first. I was either writing many different records at the one time, or I was writing one record with many different voices, different perspectives." It was not apparent to Tori Amos from the get-go that the material that would become *American Doll Posse* was speaking to her in the voices of five different women, characters she embodied in the songs and, eventually, in the album's artwork, promotion, and tour. "When the songs were coming to me before they were recorded," said Amos to g3mag.co.uk, "I began to notice that the style from one to the next was extreme in some cases. . . . I realized they were coming from different women's voices; I tried to allow my body to become clay and for them to take over. I think a lot of women, if you got them in a corner and asked them, 'Are there secret sides to you, that if you didn't have responsibilities and you could just go and investigate, would you?' I think a lot of women would say yes." The doll posse explored those sides of the artist known as Tori Amos: she introduced us to Isabel, Clyde, Pip, Santa, and Tori.

Looking at the songs from a producer's standpoint, Amos realized that "'for this to work, it's pivotal that the arrangements take it song by song, instead of as a whole record.' A lot of the time, I look at the whole work. Pieces have to work together for there to be this sonic installation. It can't just be random things thrown together, it doesn't work. Sort of like a meal where you have Japanese and Swedish and Indian and Thai, but after a while, it's just, uhhh there's no harmony in it. So that was the trick."

Inspiration for writing *American Doll Posse* came from, among other things, poetry by Rimbaud, Baudelaire, Dickinson, and Plath. Always one to look beyond the current framework of pop culture for inspiration, Tori cautioned in an interview with *American Songwriter*, "I think as a songwriter you can get trapped into writing songs that are like the ones you hear on the radio, and sometimes you want to do that and sometimes you don't, because by the time your song comes out, that'll be dated. So you have to think, 'Where am I going for my reference points?' And sure, sometimes I will hear something that makes me think, 'Well, I like the way that they were using alliteration, I like the way they are making your senses work in this song,' but you can apply it to what you're doing while making sure it comes out in a really different way. . . . [As a lyricist], I think sometimes in order for the listener to apply a story to their own life, abstraction's good for that, because it doesn't quarantine a song into your own event which is bad. In that way, there is a narcissism to that, as a songwriter. And you have to be smart. Sometimes songwriters are sitting there telling you exactly what happened." Using "Hey George" as an example of that, Amos writes about George Bush as well as King George but instead of being literal, she avoids pointing the finger: "It's a pretty intimate conversation you're having about the tragic place that we're in, a heartbreaking place. You had to get the people's emotions. Unless you permeate the place, people are very defensive of where they are with their politics. If you start pointing the finger, preaching doesn't get you very far, I don't think. But getting under people's skin, getting intimate about this subject, was the only way for this song to work."

In an interview with *American Songwriter*, Amos made clear that, at her core, she's still writing from the same place that she was when she wrote *Little Earthquakes* — from an artistic rather than commercial starting point: "As a songwriter, greatness is not measured by how many eaters of fast food there  are; there's more fast food eaters and beer drinkers than there are of good wine. So you have to know, am I making good wine, or am I making Pabst for the planet? You have to know what you're doing."

And Amos certainly does. Of her pre-production process, Marcel van Limbeek shared, "Nowadays she spends a certain amount of time writing songs, and as she's writing, she's recording demos of them too. During this process, she gets me or Mark or both of us involved, and a lot of early decisions are made then in terms of what microphones she's going to pick for certain songs, for instance. That's one thing she's always been very interested in: finding the right vocal mic for the right song. So as she's writing and doing early recording, we might swap different vocal mics to find the right one, and usually come up with some early vocal effects that might or might not make it through all the way till the end. So we come up with some early ideas of what the color should be of the production, and basically record demos of her vocal and piano, or another keyboard she might be playing. Then it's just a demo if you like, and what will happen next is the band will come in, they listen to the demo, we all talk about it, and we come up with a battle plan to record the real thing. In between, from when the band flies in and we come up with the battle plan, that's the time that me and Mark spend going through all the mics and mic pre-amps, and making sure everything sounds as good as possible. So we test all the mics, set up the drums, have one big setup day basically to get everything sounding as good as possible.

"I think for this LP, just the same as every album prior, we were looking at trying to find a different sound — just as *Choirgirl Hotel* sounded different from *Boys for Pele*, we needed a different sound from *Beekeeper* to this album. So for this album, we were aiming for a more aggressive sound. Where *Beekeeper* had been a more happy sort of sound, this was going to sound more bitey. That was definitely our approach from the start. I remember Tori talking about it even before we recorded one single note, so that was a big departure. It was a big difference because I remember that the band was rocking out, whereas previously they might have been maybe a bit more careful. Because Tori plays so dynamic and plays so soft, so for instance, the way Matt used to play used to be quite intricate, where he'd hit his toms really softly. Whereas on *American Doll Posse*, the guy was pounding. It was beautiful, and something he might not have dared to do early on. That sort of thing was a reflection of the band having become even more comfortable together. We needed a more aggressive sound, and there you have it."

Of course, Tori's piano was still central to the sound of *American Doll Posse*, and drummer Matt Chamberlain "just couldn't imagine her not playing — from knowing her as long as I have — there's just no way she's going to stop writing or playing. She's unbelievable live, and she just keeps writing, so even by the law of averages, by the fact that she produces so much music, chances are she's going to write a bunch of great songs. And at this point, she has; she's written so much material, and I've always thought she was one of those artists that people aren't going to fully appreciate till like twenty years from now. They'll go, 'Oh my God, she was writing all this while I was listening to Arcade Fire.' I think a lot of the songs she has written are unbelievable, and a lot of people don't know what the heck she's talking about, but once you get inside them and realize all that's going on, it's pretty cool, pretty unique."

Reflecting on the length of time he'd spent working with Tori at the time of *American Doll Posse*, Chamberlain said, "At the end of the last tour I was talking to her, and saying, 'Man, you know it's been ten years we've been playing together,' and I really don't play drums like I do with her with anyone else. We've developed our own vocabulary, it's pretty cool, because the way she plays and the way I play with her is unique just to that situation. Actually the way we all play together, with Jon also, the musical vocabulary we've developed is completely unique. At this point, it's so easy for all of us to work together, that's the main thing. If she wants to turn on a dime and go into a lounge-jazz groove, or record hard rock tunes, or go electro-freaky, she knows with this group of musicians, she can do that. She has a group of people who can pretty much do whatever she needs to do, and on top of that, we're all friends, so it's a big plus. There's a mutual respect, and I think you could compare it to any great job working with people, if there's a good team of people working on a project. It just makes it so much more fun, and if everyone's really good at what they do, then you can go anywhere and do anything you might need to do. You can't really complain when you get to go out to a farm, eat great food, drink great wine, and make amazing music, and have a good time. I'd definitely call it a family; for better or worse, we're a family! It's just all good.

"At this point, I just talk to her before I go out there, asking her what I should bring, really, because we're in the middle of nowhere. Then the hardest part really is: she writes so many songs; I think for *American Doll Posse*, we tracked near forty songs. So every day we'd wake up, and work on a song till it was done, so that every day was a new song. She tends to average a song a day, unless there's a technical snag, or we cut it at the wrong tempo, or it wasn't the right take on it. So there's a couple songs like that where we go back and revisit it, but usually we cut a song a day."

Offering a peek into the percussion setup in the studio for *American Doll Posse*, Chamberlain revealed, "We actually had two rooms in the studio going at once; one room was all just percussion and crazy drum things and electronics, then there was a second room which was just drum kits. So we'd bounce back and forth, and maybe I'd say, 'Hey, let me record some percussion into my laptop, then run it through this guitar pedal, then we'll make a loop out of it, then we'll play to that, and then I'll run back into the drum room and play drums to the loop I just made, and see what that sounds like.' A lot of that kind of stuff. There were definitely things that — just being a part of the group for as long as I had — I thought needed to happen, from my point of view, with my playing. A lot of it was getting more aggressive, really taking it over the top. On *Scarlet's Walk*, I'd definitely brought out the big John Bonham drums, but I didn't necessarily go full-on, which I should have. When I look back on some of those records, I'm like, 'Shit, man, it would have been great to have this extreme juxtaposition of moods going on.'

"So for *American Doll Posse*, the idea behind the album was she had all these characters, and the way I read it, all of the albums we'd done, leading up to this, were all of her different musical characters. We'd done everything from super poppy stuff to rock to electronic stuff, orchestral — it just spanned the whole range across every genre. So *American Doll Posse*, to me, seemed like she was saying, 'I'm going to write in every genre, where we're going to categorize all these songs,' so there's the rock songs, the psychedelic songs, the singer-songwriter stuff. So there were songs that are just full-on rock songs, and for those, I just went at it from that point of view. Then there were other songs where I didn't know what the hell to do, so I just would sit around in my drum room with my laptop and make up these crazy beats and loops, and then present them to her. It was a little more of a process because we were going through something, we just didn't know exactly what it was, we just wanted to leave it open to experimentation and see what could happen, as far as the drums were concerned. A lot of her songs were written already, so for me it was a matter of 'How am I going to fit into all that?' and make it sound like it made sense with what she was going for."

From a technical vantage point, Marcel van Limbeek explained that "a big difference on *American Doll Posse* is that we started using the M-S miking technique on the piano, and it worked really well. It was much better because there was so much more guitar stuff going on; it was much harder and brighter sounds. So it was much harder to mix in the piano, so we began recording it with M-S, which is basically a stereo mic technique, but different altogether. It was a stereo mic too, but with a much less phasey sound, and much more direct. Plus, you have control over the width as you mix it, and normally when you record stereo microphones, the width space is being determined by how far the mics are apart from one another. Whereas with M-S, you have control over that during mix-down, so you have a lot more control, and it worked fantastic with the piano. It was the way to do it because we had to mix it in with all those loud guitars and clashing sounds, and that's not easy with the piano, while still keeping it prominent in the mix."

Of the production team's dynamic in-studio, van Limbeek shared that the bond "between Tori and Mark, having now been married ten years, reflects trust more than anything else. They've always sort of separated their personal life from their professional life, but they definitely have a creative intuitiveness, but again Tori's definitely the guiding light. The one thing that's fair to say about all three of us — that I'm sure Mark and Tori would agree with — is that ultimately everybody realizes it's Tori's product and her name on the cover. And over the years, it never feels comfortable when either I or Mark would disagree with something, then it's not right. We always try to find a point where it works for all three of us on those few occasions where there might have been a disagreement on how to take it further. It's always Tori's call, but even in a mix session, while Tori likes to be around, very much so, but typically what will happen is she'll give me and Mark space to set up the mix, and work on it. So she won't interfere in the earlier stage, but she'll already have a good idea of what's going to happen, because we'll have had some kind of mix up during the recording process. Also, we always print rough mixes every time we do an overdub of a new instrument, we print a copy for her so she can listen to it in her own time. So even before mixing, she'll have an idea, and more than often she'll say, 'Oh by the way, that rough mix is really good,' or 'You need to work on it.' So she'll have given us a good idea of how to start off. Then she usually comes in in the early afternoon and gives her comments. In all my years, Mark and I have mixed maybe three or four songs in her absence, because she couldn't make it due to a meeting or something. And even now, I don't feel good about those songs, because she wasn't there, and even though she said she loved them and they were great, it still didn't feel complete. It's funny how that is."

Though the band and production team had been working with Tori for a decade, the sound they produced on *American Doll Posse* was fresh. Released in April 2007, *American Doll Posse* was hailed by *Rolling Stone* as "Amos's best album in many years," while *Spin* described it as "not merely the most confrontational, catchy, and guitar-heavy music of Tori Amos's career, [but] arguably the singer-pianist's greatest, and undeniably sexiest, album." Though the album encompassed five distinct personalities via her doll posse, as a whole it was undeniably and unmistakably the artistry of Tori Amos.

"A successful songwriting moment for me is when I'm not trying to write something for a demographic, for a format, and yet people have a truly emotional response to it."

— TORI AMOS (*PERFORMING SONGWRITER*, 2009)

CHAPTER 12

Abnormally Attracted to Sin and *Midwinter Graces* (2009)

Finding time in her busy touring and recording schedule to devote herself to projects outside her normal sphere — such as collaborating on 2008's *Comic Book Tattoo*, a collection of stories in comic-book form inspired by Amos's music — Tori happened upon a phrase that would become the title of her next studio album. While researching musicals for her stage adaptation of George MacDonald's fairytale *The Light Princess*, which she was working on with Samuel Adamson, Amos re-watched *Guys and Dolls*. "[The character of Sarah Brown is] a repressed religious girl. I know those very well," Tori told *Time Out*. "It was a jumping-off point; when I saw *Guys and Dolls* again, and I heard that line ["abnormally attracted to sin"], I stopped and I knew. I just knew. I've just gone into another dimension of what this means."

Her first studio project under a new distribution pact with Universal Republic included an accompanying video, or "visualette," for each track on the album. Rather than acting as a bonus feature made as an afterthought to the project, the visualettes guided much of her songwriting. Videographer Christian Lamb had originally been hired by her previous label to film her while on tour. Explained Amos to *American*

Songwriter, "This all got started because we were doing something else. Life happens while you're doing something that you didn't plan. He jumped on board the bus on the West Coast. We were filming the live show and he was doing pick-up camera work all the way down the coast. I would be shown these little vignettes that he would put together along with live recordings, music from one of the shows, that night and I said, 'Cut this off, let's turn the music off. This is wrong.' And I'd look at them and there was another story. I think he was filming at a certain point in the tour when the world was changing; it was the crest of the crash. It was the crest of things, our world that changed overnight was just beginning this shift. So the songs were written in stages. There was that group. But some of the songs were not 'inspired' only by the visuals I saw. Some of them were coming from things that were happening so fast, the changes, and then he would go away and think about 'Do we have visuals for this?' I didn't know I was making a project with sixteen short films."

The project was a "definite collaboration" with Lamb in terms of creating these videos, and for Amos, it was a natural progression as she's always been inspired by visual arts. "I am influenced by visual artists quite a bit. I can hear things when I see . . . I think it pushes me further to interpret something that isn't my art form," explained Amos to *Buzzine,* "and then I can bring what I discover to my art form. They point me in directions that get me to hear things that I haven't heard before. . . . I stay away from current music when I walk into full-form composition, but I surround myself with visual art that I collect around the world — art books, information . . . It's kind of central to my composing."

In an interview with Amazon.com, Amos reasoned that her music was an immersive experience — particularly *Abnormally Attracted to Sin*: "I create worlds for you to walk into. I'm not creating a little pile of leaves for you to jump into, I'm creating a forest of sound. Some architects build cottages, some build cathedrals. I'm more interested in that shape where things are interconnected. It's not just about a poem that lives on its own. There are people who are wonderful at that form. But I'm making the whole installation, not just the postcard. I'm not saying I don't love postcards, but I like getting involved in something that takes me to another world for a long time." Inspiration from "the muse" came for Tori at any moment — unexpected or planned — but with this album it was often while traveling that she was particularly prolific: "It can be

Tori Amos Abnormally Attracted To Sin

when I'm taking a shower, sitting having a coffee somewhere, and she walks in, in a dream in the middle of the night — a lot of the time when I'm traveling, because your senses are heightened and you're out of it. I just resolve myself to the muse being in control." To Amazon.com, she expanded on that point, "A lot of energy was put into different compositional styles [for this album]. I started composing when I was out on the road this last time. And when I travel I usually get these waves of — I don't know — songs coming to visit me. And maybe because you're out with different influences, and your senses are getting aroused in a beautiful way, sometimes you're not feeling in your safe zone, so you start thinking about things you might not think about in your normal routine."

Of her composition process, Tori explained, "The songs are there before the guys [start] working on it. So the songs have developed. Sometimes it's a phrase, a lyric that has found its way all the way here and I start singing and humming around it. Or sometimes I get a musical passage and I think to myself, 'This isn't just a bit of salt, this is something that I need to base something on. This is the heart and soul to a composition.' You just have to learn to the read the signs. You're getting inspiration all the time. Sometimes it doesn't seem to click but it's there."

As Amos developed this album, she discovered her songs didn't have one particular sound but rather revisited all the various sounds she had explored on previous albums. Speaking to Pressetext.com,

Amos said, "Because the compositions were so diverse, it sort of set the blueprints for the building. Early on, Mark and I were hammering out concepts for arrangements. Then Mark and Marcel were hammering out sonic direction, so when all the players came in, they would be working within the blueprints. After having done *American Doll Posse*, for which I needed to have a more of a band kind of feeling in production, something like this was encompassing twenty years of my composition style. Even though it wasn't going back to *From the Choirgirl Hotel* it grabs styles from each period of my career."

Bringing in the ideas of her production team and musicians brought out the producer in Tori. As she told *Buzzine*, "I started fooling around with them and the production side of my brain . . . well, everything has changed because of the building of the sounds, and a library was developed, of the sounds, which started long before we recorded. Maybe the difference between now and many, many years ago is that I understand how involved producing is. There's a lot that happens in post-production, and before, when you don't know all the possibilities, sometimes you don't explore them either — you just take the obvious route, and that doesn't mean you can't make a good record, but it might not be a record that's making you think of 'listen to what that's doing, and listen to all those layers and listen to what's happening here.' So time was spent on it. I enjoy being in the studio and working with teams of people because, in that way, you have sounding boards and you have people that will get you through it, and then you can find the right answer when there are enough people in the room with different points of view."

That team was back in Cornwall to record at Martian Engineering with the Bösendorfer and the touring band: guitarist Mac Aladdin (Mark Hawley's guitar-playing alter ego), bassist Jon Evans, and Matt Chamberlain. Amos wrote songs that she hoped would challenge and inspire her fellow musicians: "I create a composition that can hold the other instruments. The musicians themselves are very much collaborators. The string arranger, bass, drums, guitars — they all bring so much to the records so that if I don't write compositions . . . how do I explain it? There are some singer-songwriters who, if you're producing them, you bring in drums, bass, and guitar to back them up. You are not bringing in these great musicians to come in and be at the forefront . . . . [and be] absolutely pushed to the limit of their musicianship. They are told to rein in most of the time. They are back-up musicians, even if they're the best in the world. The last couple records have been about 'I have to write music that challenges them.' This can't just be about 'you fit around my piano playing and this is the center.' No, the song is the center. And if the piano isn't the instrument that best expresses the song, then give the piano player a break and let the others come forth."

Speaking to *The Advocate*, Amos admitted, "My interest in [experimentation] has grown over the years. . . . I realized that [my] records have not centered on the piano for a while. I think that if they would have, I wouldn't have the career that I have. I wouldn't have grown as a composer. I will do a record [again] where the piano is the center, but I needed to grow as a composer, because at a certain point my structures started becoming repetitive. And I recognize this. So I started to infiltrate my brain with George Martin arrangements, all the Beatles records, and others . . . all kinds of records from all kinds of times. I always thought of myself as a composer first, never a pianist. I mean, I'm good, I'm okay. And so I didn't just want to write piano music, I wanted to write compositions for the musicians where Jon and Matt and John Philip [strings] would turn around and say, 'Wow.' Sort of like an architect with these plans to build the World Trade Center. You're stepping out of your safe zone when you're not just building beautiful houses. You say no. You build these places that have many rooms that interconnect, and as a composer, I began to see, 'Okay, I've been building planets,' then you build solar systems, and then you want to build a galaxy." Another challenge was making a record with such a variety of sounds compared to more straightforward albums Amos had recorded previously: "Honestly, we had quite a hard time doing it, because there are so many different styles. The electronic side, then the big strings, it was like going to many different shows at fashion week."

The singer explained to Popmatters.com that so many years of tireless performing around the world had changed her voice and how aware she is of her instrument: "Sometimes listening back to how you're using your voice, with the bootlegs and things like that, can make you aware of 'Well, when I do this, and it feels like this, it *sounds* like that.' And so, over the years, it has changed, getting older, in a certain way. Maybe touring so much, I think the instrument; I work with it a lot. I think maybe if I didn't tour so much, the instrument wouldn't be growing and changing. You know how if some people don't tour, they don't use their instrument a lot? If you use it a lot, then you get to develop, it gets strong, and you begin to know how to handle it better."

Delving into the creation of some of the album's tracks, Tori shared that "Maybe California" came to her "when I was seeing mothers — not just one — ask the question that if they weren't there anymore, would it just be the better answer for the family? And when I started to really understand the gravity of what that meant . . . because these aren't women who are crazy; these are just women pushed to a point [who] can't fix the tragedies that happen to families, where they've lost everything and can't put their kids through college and the husband's lost the job, and it goes on." Amos saw that in pop culture "it's glamorous to talk about the struggle of teenagers surviving those challenges, and people in their early twenties. But the idea that our backbone of society, our nurturing mothers, is starting to fall apart." Amos invoked the tragic figure of Ophelia for her song about "a woman who is drawn to situations — I would say not just men but situations — where somebody needs to have control over her in some way, and she hasn't been able to break the chain of these people. They seem to come in different forms in her life. So until you yourself begin to know, 'Why am I attracted to people who are like this?' then you can't break free. Sometimes you're not willing to look at this characteristic in them; you're not willing to see it for some reason. And that's the story of 'Ophelia.'" In "Police Me," Amos explored "the whole idea of remote viewing and how people analyze each other through information and email." Amos explained to PopMatters.com that "Lady in Blue" tells the story of a love that endures but doesn't work out: "in the end, she has her music and she recognizes that that is the resolve. He is not going to run off with her, but he still loves her. I felt that was important to the song, that it doesn't give you that Disney ending, because life, a lot of times, isn't like that."

As was now a regular occurrence, Tori's album debuted in the top 10 of the Billboard Top 200 Album chart in May 2009, and while she toured in support of it, she had yet another LP in the works that would be released before the year was out — the surprising collection that made up Amos's holiday album, *Midwinter Graces*.

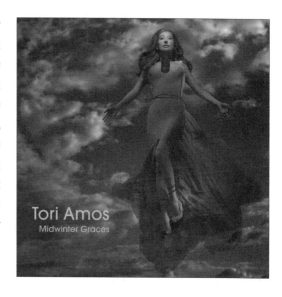

* * *

For most artists two decades into their career, a Christmas album comes off as a little bit desperate and bears little to no originality. In Amos's unique fashion, she created a "Christmas album" unlike any other, giving fans five originals along with more traditional fare reimagined.

The idea for the album originated with Universal Music Group CEO Doug Morris, who Amos reconnected with after years apart when he lured her from Epic to Universal. Related the singer, "[He] said to me, 'I'm seventy years old, Tori, I want you to do a seasonal record; you're a minister's daughter. Just don't make it overly religious.' I said that happens naturally and he said, 'Don't offend your mother, but don't offend me either.'" Her parents had, in fact, long wanted her to do a holiday album, Amos told Virgin.com, "but they wanted it to be true to all the hymns that they hold dear. But that didn't interest me. The good thing is that they have embraced the record and it hasn't offended them. I didn't make this to offend them. I wanted to widen up the ideology, so it wasn't just for Christian believers but for people that may be spiritual in some way." Amos quipped to *Gay Calgary*, "I think the fact that I didn't write 'She's a Hussy, Merry Christmas' all made everybody really happy. There's no mention of Satan or dancing with Satan or anything like that. There's nothing disrespectful on this record; it's really beautiful."

With no interest in making "a cliché record," Amos said of other holiday albums that artists are often "just doing covers of tunes that you've heard a million times. This has new versions and new songs." To write the new material for the album, Tori admitted, "You have to have certain emotions that you are feeling put in a context that works. You get nostalgic memories of people that aren't with you anymore. You go to find them and they are not there, whether they have left the planet or are not in your life anymore. A lot of people share that experience."

Tori was making a record that's less about the birth of Christ and "more about the rebirth of the sun, the birth of light"; Amos told Metro. co.uk, "Our ancestors have been celebrating midwinter time for thousands of years all over the world, long before Christianity. Some of the music is beautiful, these carols, but they took it from other places and made it religious." Interest in midwinter celebrations was nothing new to Amos: "I've been reading about the solstices ever since I was twelve or thirteen years old, and I asked a lot of questions about how our ancestors would celebrate this time before Christianity. I was really fascinated. It's just been one of those things that I've been collecting different information about for over thirty years. So all of that served me when I embraced the idea of a seasonal album." Speaking to NYmag. com about the album, Amos pointed out that the tradition of reimagining hymns and spiritual songs was also nothing new: "Some of [these songs] go back so far. And what would happen is, these new denominations would be popping up and they'd think, 'Oh, God, we need some hit songs.' So they'd take a popular song and put Christology to it. I've carried on the tradition. I've done variations of the themes that were variations of the themes." Amos's rewrites were not done on a whim; rather, "in order to make this kind of record and to have it work, I needed to know what the carol writers were doing, then you need to know the theology of where it came from in order to change it. I did change it in making it more inclusive rather than exclusive." To *Keyboard*, she put it simply: "I would look at portions of a carol and think, 'Wow, this is the magic. Now I need to design around this.'"

Amos's years at the Peabody came into play while creating this album, both in providing musicians to play in the strings section and in terms of her training being put to good use. "[Studying classical music] gives you tools that you don't necessarily get to use all the time when you're in the pop medium," Tori told *Keyboard*. "But when you're dealing with something like this and you're treading on very thin ice and sacred ground in some ways, to know that variations on a theme is just part of the classical world [is important], and I enjoy working and composing variations around a theme. You just have to make sure that your variations are as good as the old ones, and you have to know when you don't have it and when you do. I began to see the reactions from the musicians when they were excited." Before recording at Martian Engineering, "[representatives from] Bösendorfer came down and gave the recording piano this gorgeous makeover, which was important because you hear the piano a lot on this work, and she shines," said Amos. Though she also played the harpsichord and recruited a big band, a string section, and a children's choir, Amos's piano playing was the center of the album in a way it hadn't been in years.

In terms of percussion, Amos told MusicRadar.com, "The key was getting the right instruments. We got in things like concert bass drums, concert bells in two octaves, tubular bells — all kinds of percussive things so Matt had the correct palette to work from. That was the key: finding him the right ingredients and taking him off the kit pretty much. But the bed was made from classical percussion, and that's why it worked." One new addition to Amos's recording team was her daughter Natashya, who contributed vocals to "Holly, Ivy and Rose." Explained Amos, "It all began because my niece, Kelsey Dobyns, who is seventeen, sings on 'Candle: Coventry Carol,' and I think Tash was fascinated with that process. She had come up with the idea to do a bit of a bawdy song, and I said, 'No, I don't think that's appropriate.' [laughs] So she said, 'Will you come up with something that is appropriate, Mummy?' And I said, 'Yeah, let me work on it.'" The two girls were not Tori's only relatives on the album; her nephew posed as the angel in its artwork. "So the next generation is represented," said Amos.

The decision to reimagine "Silent Night" into "A Silent Night with You" came from Doug Morris. Said Amos, "Doug really encouraged me to do this. He talked to me a lot about feelings he had when he would listen to the carols, and he said that sometimes they wouldn't bring him to a religious place; they'd bring him to a nostalgic place. We talked about this particular idea, and I went away thinking, 'My mother is going to lose her mind if I do anything to "Silent Night"!' . . . [But] she loves this song. She adores it." One of Amos's original winter-themed compositions for the album, "A Winter's Carol," came from another project she had on the go, the adaptation of *The Light Princess*. "I did a version that's kind of 'Tori-fied.' I was thrilled that the Children's Choir in New York, P.S. 122, did a version of it. I was in tears when I saw the children singing it because I thought, 'That's right — it's supposed to be a choral arrangement.' And children will be singing it in *The Light Princess*. It just worked out. It was as if the director of the Children's Choir knew what it should be." Of her take on "We Three Kings," Amos quipped, "We need a little Led Zeppelin on 'Star of Wonder.'"

In an interview with *Keyboard*, Amos described the recording process: "I played for John Philip Shenale, talked him through my vision, and he really got it. I tracked it with the guys first — Matt and Jon — and they got a sense of the rhythm. We laid down the rhythm track first with the Wurlitzer, and that gave it that early Zeppelin sound. Then we brought in everything that you could possibly imagine percussion-wise for Matt to play, from tympanis to concert bass drums, two octaves of concert bells, along with his kit and all the other ethnic percussion. Matt had a huge palette to work with, which was exciting. So 'Star of Wonder' has that flavor — you'll recognize the carol in the chorus. But it has beautiful dancing girls now. In my seasonal world, I think beautiful dancing girls celebrating the rebirth of light — in the Christian story, the poetry for that is the birth of a baby boy. But the rebirth of light that happens every year has been celebrated by our ancestors for thousands of years and I wanted to capture that."

Upon its release in November 2009, Amos's second new album in a year was an instant hit with fans and critics alike, with the *New York Times* calling it "gorgeously recorded and impeccably produced." For Tori, *Midwinter Graces* carried with it a message of light: "[T]his time of year, if you're in our hemisphere, is about the rebirth of light.

But light means knowledge, light means consciousness. Everybody can attain that and have that in their life. Consider the idea that it's inner God. It's in every child that's born; every child carries this ability within them. And I like that sentiment."

Conclusion

Back in 1994, Tori Amos told *Performing Songwriter* that her need to create music is innate, and she would perform whether or not it was also her career: "I just kept honoring myself. I said, this is what I do, I'm a girl who plays the piano. This is what I do. So if nobody comes to see me, guess what, I'll be in my living room playing the piano. Now I hustled and I got my work out there and it's not like I didn't take it to the street, because I did. I played for as many people as I could and I keep honing my craft and I keep trying to just explore myself and explore my writing and share it." Nearly 20 years after the release of *Under the Pink*, Tori Amos has stayed true to her course — tirelessly writing, recording, touring, and captivating audiences with her inimitable style, which evolves and shifts from album to album but is constant in its Tori-ness.

On the subject of Tori's importance to music and how she fits in, longtime drummer Matt Chamberlain said, "People are always trying to pigeon-hole her, but she's disproven everybody's theories. She just keeps going and going, and I think the more records she puts out, she'll continue to show people she's a force. I mean, my next record with her is a musical. . . . I love the fact that it's different every time and an adventure, and an opportunity to make music with someone who's really talented, and it's always a learning experience too. I do so many records [with other artists] where you're just kind of playing and thinking, 'What's the point in putting this record out into the world?' As a session player, I think that a lot about people I will not name, but with her, always I go, 'Man, I'm so glad that she's making records,' because there's nobody like her doing this.'"

At the time of writing, Amos is at work on her first musical, *The Light Princess*, set to debut in spring 2012 at London's National Theatre, but that project hasn't stopped her from touring, releasing live albums, and collaborating with other recording artists. In a culture increasingly full of knockoffs and imitators, Tori Amos's unyielding originality and refusal to rest on her laurels has deservedly earned her a place in the pantheon of alternative music as well as legions of devoted fans who will turn up to hear whatever it is she comes up with next. As Tori said in a recent radio interview, "I've had a big career and a long career and I'm still going."

SOURCES

Aaron, Charles. "Sex, God, and Rock 'N' Roll." *Spin*. October 1994.

Abubakar, Pearlsha. "The Scarlet Letter." *Pulp*. January/February 2003.*

Alber, Rebecca. "Tori Story." *Curve*. September 1996.*

Ali, Lorraine. "Tori Amos." *Us*. December 1996.*

Allan, Vicky. "Under the Covers." *Scotland on Sunday*. December 2, 2001.*

Alper, Aaron. "A Chat with Tori Amos." *Tampa Bay Times*. August 10, 2005.*

Alteri, Suzan. "Tori Amos: Undercover." *Real Detroit Weekly*. September 15, 2001.*

"Amos Takes Leaders to Task with Album." ninemsn.com.au. February 12, 2005.*

Andersson, Eric. "Tori's Turn." *MetroSource*. February/March 2003.*

Andrews, Lea. "American Doll." g3mag.co.uk. April 2007.*

"Around Time." *Recording Musician*. March 2005.*

"Artist Snapshot: Tori Amos." encore.celebrityaccess.com. May 26, 2009.

Ashare, Matt. "Conversation Pieces." *Boston Phoenix*. April 8–14, 2005.*

Ayers, Michael D. "Tori Amos on How and Why She Made a Christmas Album." NYMag.com. November 11, 2009.

Azzopardi, Chris. "Merry . . . Midwinter?" *GayCalgary and Edmonton Magazine*. November 2009.

Bailie, Stuart. "Song of the Month: 'Talula' by Tori Amos." *Vox*. May 1996.*

Balfour, Brad. "What Really Gets to You?" *The New Review of Records*. 1994.*

Barnes, Ken. "Travels with Tori." *Music Central*. March 17, 1997.*

Beal Jr., Jim. "Amos' Latest 'Walk' More of a Meander." *San Antonio Express-News*. April 25, 2003.*

Bennett, James. "The Big Interview: No Pain, No Gain." *The Times*. April 11, 1998.

Benson, Leslie. "Abnormally attracted to Tori Amos." Nuvo.net.

Bialczak, Mark. "America Is a Character in This." *The Post-Standard*. February 28, 2003.*

"Biografie: Tori Amos." ThePop.de. February 2005.*

Blackman, Guy. "The Whole Tori." *The Age*. May 8, 2005.*

Blackwood, Alisa. "Songwriter and her manager form their own label." *Indiana Daily Student*. November 14, 1996.*

Blandford, James R. "Tales of the Bee Mistress." *Record Collector*. November 2006.*

Bledsoe, Wayne. "Tori Amos' Press Kit Is as Big as a Book." *Knoxville News-Sentinel*. August 14, 1998.*

Block, Francesca Lia. "Tori Amos: The Volcano Lover." *Spin*. March 1996.*

Bosso, Joe. "Tori Amos on Her New Holiday Album *Midwinter Graces*." MusicRadar.com. December 8, 2009.

Boyd, Brian. "Soul Searching." *The Irish Times*. November 2, 2002.*

Breen, Matthew. "The Tori Amos Album You Never Expected." Advocate.com. November 10, 2009.

Britt, Bruce. "Amos Feeling in the 'Pink.'" *Time Out*. February 11, 1994.

Brown, Glyn. "On the Road with the Tori Party." *The Times*. December 18, 2001.*

Brown, Mark. "America at Her Gait." *Rocky Mountain News*. December 4, 2002.*

Brown, G. "Tori Amos' Great American Journey." *Denver Post*. December 4, 2002.*

Buitenhuis, Eugene. "Tori Amos Spits Fire." *Veronica*. May 7–13, 1994.*

Cahill, Phillippe. "On the Couch with . . . Tori Amos." *Campaign*. December 1994.*

Campbell, Chuck. "Moody Music." *Chicago Tribune*. October 8, 1992.*

Campbell, Mary. "Songwriter's Work Explores Inner Self." Associated Press. April 5, 1994.

Carvalho, Hester. "My Best Work Comes Sailing into Me Like a Spirit." *NRC Handelblad*. January 31, 1994.*

Catlin, Roger. "Amos Revealed with Personal Songs and Political Action." *Hartford Courant*. July 10, 1994.*

———. "Tori in Her Glory." *The Hartford Courant*. October 11, 2001.*

Chandar, Chris. "Tori Amos." *Pulse!* November 2002.*

Che, Cathy. "Who's Tori Now?" *Time Out New York*. May 1996.*

Christensen, Thor. "Rebel, Well . . ." *Dallas Morning News*. June 14, 1996.*

Clark, Rob. "Travels with Tori." *Dallas Morning News*. April 18, 2003.*

Cohen, Howard. "What Is Tori Amos Talking About?" *Fort Lauderdale Herald*. April 12, 1996.*

Cole, Susan G. "Tori Amos Baring Her Soul in the Name of Art." *Now*. July 23–29, 1998.

Coleman, Nick. "Vote Tori." *Time Out*. January 22–29, 1992.*

Condran, Ed. "A Darker Side of 'Pink.'" *Asbury Park Press*. August 22, 2003.*

———. "Her Stamp on Men's Words." *The Record*. October 5, 2001.*

———. "In Her Memoir and Album, Amos Reveals a Bit of Herself." *Orlando Sentinel*. April 1, 2005.*

Conner, Thomas. "Tori Amos Compares Rock to Classical in the Context of Jimi Hendrix, Ripples in a River . . . and Stinky Cheese." *Tulsa World News*. November 1, 1996.*

Considine, J.D. "The Feminine Musique." *Baltimore Sun*. January 21, 1996.*

———. "Touring with Tori." *Baltimore Sun*. September 26, 1996.*

———. "Tori Amos Follows Up 'Little Earthquakes' With Another Album Aftershock." *Baltimore Sun*. January 30, 1994.*

———. "Tori Amos Takes the Road Less Traveled." *Baltimore Morning Sun*. July 22, 1994.*

———. "With a New Sound, Amos Appears Poised for Solid-Gold Stardom." *The Baltimore Sun*. May 29, 1998.*

———. Transcript of interview with Tori Amos. *Baltimore Sun*. January 30, 1994.

Crain, Zac. "Still Orbiting." *Dallas Observer*. September 22, 1999.*

Cromelin, Richard. "Tori Amos' Emotional Richter Scale." *Los Angeles Times*. May 11, 1992.

Cummins, Kevin. "Tori Seems to Be the Hardest Need." *NME*. December 17, 1994.

Curtis, Jonathan. "Girls on Film: An Interview with Tori Amos." AmericanSongwriter.com. May 15, 2009.

D'Angelo, Joe. "Tori Amos Writes Scarlet Letters, Draws Tour Map." MTV. com September 23, 2002.

Daley, David. "Magic & Loss." *Alternative Press*. July 1998.

Daly, Steven. "Tori Amos: Her Secret Garden." *Rolling Stone*. June 25, 1998.

Danton, Eric R. "Amos Sees Americans Awakening." *Hartford Courant*. November 15, 2002.*

Darling, Andy. "Victim in Search of Her True Voice." *The Guardian*. November 1991.*

Davies, Mike. "Breaking the Silence." *What's On Birmingham*. December 21, 1991.*

Davis, Tim C. "Strange Little Girl." *Creative Loafing*. October 3–9, 2001.*

Dawn, Randee. "Is Tori Amos Bullshit?" *Alternative Press*. October 2001.*

——. "Venus Envy." *Alternative Press*. October 1999.*

De Bottom, Alain. "Tori Amos." *Vogue* (Germany). September 2001.*

De Yampert, Rick. "Tori Amos Fills Choirgirl Hotel with Mythic Metaphors." *The Tennessean*. August 23, 1998.

Deevoy, Adrian. "Hips. Lips. Tits. Power." Q. May 1994.

DeFretos, Lydia Carole. "Tori Amos: Finding Her Own Fire." *Aquarian Weekly*. February 21, 1996.

DeMain, Bill. "Mother of Invention." *Performing Songwriter*. January/February 2002.

——. "The Inner World of Tori Amos." *Performing Songwriter*. March/April 1994.

DeSantis, Carla A. "Tori Amos: Notes From a Life." *The Seattle Times*. September 10, 1998.*

——. "Tori Amos: The Crispy Cornflake Girl." *Rockrgrl*. November/December 1998.

Devaney, Scott. "Cornflake Girl." *The Wave*. April 10–23, 2003.*

DeYoung, Bill. "Tori Amos." *Stuart News*. August 29, 2003.*

Diehl, Matt. "Stories for Girls." *Elle*. September 2001.

Dillon, Cathy. "Bigger Earthquakes." *Hot Press*. February 1996.*

DiMartino, Dave. "The Story of Tori." *Launch*. 1996.*

Divola, Barry. "Neverending Tori." *Yen*. June/July 2005.*

Dodson, Kyle. "Tori's Course on Creativity." Transcript. February 27, 1995.*

Doerschuk, Robert L. "Take a Dance Through Childhood . . ." *All Music*. October 1999.*

——. "Tori Amos: Dancing with the Vampire and The Nightingale." *Keyboard*. November 1994.*

———. "Voices In The Air: Spirit Tripping with Tori Amos." *Musician*. May 1996.*

Downie, Stephen. "Wild Honey." *The Advertiser*. May 12, 2005.*

Doyle, Tom. "Ready, Steady . . . Kook!" *Q*. May 1998.

Dunlevy, T'Cha. "Tori's Weird World." *Montreal Gazette*. August 24, 2005.*

Dunn, Bill. "A Date with Tori Amos." *Esquire*. October 1999.

Dunn, Jancee. "Q & A." *Rolling Stone*. September 30, 1999.

———. "Tori Amos." *Rolling Stone*. October 31, 2002.

Dwyer, Michael. "On an Ungodly Mission." *The West Australian*. August 11, 1994.*

Economou, Alexandra. "Tori's Tale." *The Advertiser* (Australia). November 29, 2003.*

Edmonds, Ben. "Sex and the Single Pianist." *Creem*. March 1994.*

Edwards, Mark. "Devil Woman." *The Face*. October 1994.*

Edwars, Mark. "A Lionness in the Confessional." *High Life*. May 1998.*

Eisner, Ken. "Tori Amos — Even When She's Looking, She Still Steps in It." *The Georgia Straight*. July 1996.*

Elfman, Lauren. "Tori Amos Interview." Buzzine via undented.com. August 3, 2009.

Ellen, Barbara. "Ginger Nut." *NME*. January 11, 1992.

"Emotionally Unavailable." *Mojo*. March 1994.*

Everson, John. "Still Going Down . . . Honestly." *Illinois Entertainer*. September 1998.*

———. "Tori Amos: Tight Socks and Feminist Freedom." *Free Music Monthly*. August 1994.*

Falik, Adam. "Strange Little Tori." RollingStone.com. October 4, 2001.

"Famous Amos: The thinking fan's Madonna." *Elle*. March 1996.*

Farley, Christopher John. "Tori, Tori, Tori!" *Time*. May 11, 1998.

Ferber, Lawrence. "Scarlet Fever." Newsweekly.com. November 20, 2002.*

Ferguson, Wm. "She-Creature of the Hollywood Hills." *Spin*. March 1994.

Ferrucci, Patrick. "Tori! Tori! Tori!" *New Haven Register*. April 7, 2005.*

Flick, Larry. "Tori Amos Shares Life Lessons." *Billboard*. March 28, 1992.

Foster, Richard. "When Tori Amos wants to escape . . ." *The Roanoke Times Online*. October 8, 1996.*

Fowley, Kim. "So you found a girl who thinks really deep thoughts . . ." *BAM*. March 11, 1994.*

France, Kim. "Sexual Healing." *Us*. February 1994.*

———. "The Cornflake Girl Grows Up." *Spin*. May 1998.

Freeman, Paul. "Tori Amos: Soul Music." *Chicago Sun-Times*. September 24, 1998.*

Freydkin, Donna. "Tori Amos' Gods and Monsters." CNN Online. September 29, 1999.

Fricke, David. "Strange Little Girls." *Rolling Stone*. September 18, 2001.

Fuss, Birgit. "Q&A: Tori Amos." *Rolling Stone* (Germany). October 2002.*

Gabriella. "Tori Amos." *The Inside Connection*. June 1998.*

Gallant, Michael. "Tori Amos Hits with Hammonds." *Keyboard*. July 2005.

——. "Tori Amos: Roots and Reinvention on *Midwinter Graces*." *Keyboard* via toribr.blogspot.com. December 1, 2009.

Gamboa, Glenn. "He Said, She Said." *Newsday*. October 7, 2001.

Garcia, Sandra A. "Tori Amos: In the Name of the Mother." *B-Side*. April/May 1994.*

——. "Tori Amos: The Woman Who Would Be King." *B-Side*. May/June 1996.*

Gardner, Elysa. "Amos' 'Walk' Goes in Search of America's Soul." *USA Today*. October 31, 2002.*

——. "Tori Amos' Personal Sphere." *USA Today*. October 1, 1999.

Gatta, John Patrick. "It's a Free Will Planet." *Magical Blend*. January 1999.*

Gee, Mike. "The Way to a Young Girl's Heart." *On the Street*. January 29, 1996.*

Ghorbani, Liza. "Tori's Story." *New York Post*. February 20, 2005.

Giles, Jeff. "Tori the Subversive." *Newsweek*. February 19, 1996.*

Gold, Kerry. "A Mystical and Mighty Artist." *Ottawa Citizen*. February 8, 2003.*

Goodman, Eleanor. "Tori Amos." bizarremag.com. December 2009.

Graff, Gary. "Q&A with Tori Amos." *The Music Monitor*. October 2002.*

——. "Sound Off." *Wall of Sound*. September 1999.*

——. "Staying Creative." *The Plain Dealer*. August 26, 2005.*

——. "The Thoughtful World of Tori Amos." *The Plain Dealer*. August 16, 2003.*

——. "Tori Amos Prefers to Take the Road Less Traveled." *The Sacramento Bee*. August 30, 1992.

——. "Tori Amos." *Wall of Sound*. April 1998.

——. "Writing Book Inspires Tori Amos' New Album." *Cleveland Plain Dealer*. February 24, 2005.*

Gray, Christopher. "Scarlet Fever." *Austin Chronicle*. April 25, 2003.*

Greene, Graeme. "Tori Amos interview: I'll run for president if Sarah Palin does." Metro.co.uk. December 21, 2009.

Gulla, Bob. "A Walk on the Wild Side." *Women Who Rock*. Fall 2002.*

Guzzetta, Marli. "Scarlet Fever." *The New Times*. March 20, 2003.*

Haiken, Melanie. "Pop Goes the Prodigy." *Piano and Keyboard*. May/June 1993.*

Hall, Dave. "Tori Amos: Exposes Her Hidden Corners." *Jam Entertainment News*. July 22, 1994.*

Hampson, Sarah. "Tori Amos: Certainly Weird, Also Shrewd." *Globe and Mail*. February 26, 2005.

Harrington, Richard. "Finally, A Prodigy Finds Her Song." *The Washington Post*. March 22, 1992.

——. "Tori Amos, In the Pink." *The Washington Post*. June 20, 1994.

——. "Tori Amos, Local Legend." *The Washington Post*. May 17, 1998.

Harrison, Malcolm. "Songs from the Soul." *Keyboard Review*. February 1992.*

Henry, Lindsey. "Death in Mexican Desert Haunted, Inspired Tori Amos." *The Charlotte Observer*. September 17, 1999.*

Herman, Maureen. "Can a Notoriously Idiosyncratic Artist Find Happiness with Her First Real Band?" *Musician*. July 1998.*

Hermes, Will. "Don't Mess with Mother Nature." *Spin*. October 2001.

——. "My Life in Music." *Spin*. November 2002.

Hersey, Brook. "Listen to Tori Amos." *Glamour*. August 1992.*

Hibbert, Tom. "Tori Amos." *Details*. November 1992.

Hill, Michael. "Stars, Planets, Wine and Song." VH1.com. 1999.

Hiltbrand, David. "Counting the Pieces of Tori Amos' World." *Philadelphia Inquirer*. February 22, 2005.*

Hochman, Steve. "Tori Amos Offers a Woman's-Eye View of Songs by Men." *Los Angeles Times*. July 1, 2001.

Hodgkinson, Will. "A Few of My Favourite Things." *The Guardian*. December 5, 2003.*

Horan, Anthony. Transcript of interview. November 2, 1994.

——. Transcript of interview. *Beat Magazine*. July 1994.*

Horowitz, K. "Telephone Interview with Tori Amos." yessaid.com. October 30, 1996.

"How Do I Look?" *The Independent* (UK). October 19, 2002.*

Hunter, James. "From the Choirgirl Hotel." *Rolling Stone*. April 16, 1998.

Iley, Chrissey. "Tori and the Hardest Words." *High Life*. November 2001.*

"Inner Walk." *Keyboard* (France). April 2003.*

"Interview: Tori Amos." Uncut.net. February 2005.*

Irvine, Susan. "Talk of the Devil." *Dazed and Confused*. February 1996.*

Ives, Brian. "Tori Amos: Wish You Were Here." VH1.com. October 28, 2002.

Jackson, Blair. "Tori Amos: In the Studio and On the Road." *Mix.* November 1996.*

Jackson, Joe. "The Hurt Inside." *Hot Press.* February 23, 1994.

———. "Tori's Story." *Hot Press.* 1992.*

Jacobs, Jay S. "Tori Amos." *Philly Rock Guide.* December 1992.*

James, Eric. "Venus Envy — The Parallel Universe of Tori Amos." *Boyz.* November 6, 1999.*

Jane, Sarah. "Tori Amos." *Diva.* March 2005.

———. "Tori Amos." *Diva.* March 2005.*

Jasmin, Ernest A. "Mystic Figures Inspire Amos." *The News Tribune.* April 22, 2005.*

Jasper, Tony. "Is Tori the Next Star?" *Manchester Evening News.* December 1991.*

Jeckell, Barry A. "Amos Embarking on Solo Piano Tour." Billboard.com. February 17, 2005.

———. "Amos Expresses Herself with New Album, Book." *Billboard.* February 11, 2005.

Johnson, Kevin C. "Healing Through Song." *Akron Beacon Journal.* September 12, 1996.*

Johnson, Troy. "People Are Strange." *Slamm.* October 31, 2001.*

Jordan, Isamu. "Shared Journey." *The Spokesman-Review.* April 4, 2003.*

Jurek, Thom. "American Doll Posse." AllMusic.com. June 2007.

Kennedy, Dana. "Next Big Tortured Chanteuse." *Entertainment Weekly.* February 18, 1994.*

Kinsey, Michelle. "Like an Open Book: Singer Tori Amos Has Little to Hide." *The Star Press.* September 18, 1996.*

Kiser, Amy. "Are You There, God? It's Me, Tori." *Westword.* August 27–September 2, 1998.*

Kolson, Ann. "Tori Amos: Long Struggle Yields an Emotional Rebirth." *The Sacramento Bee.* May 8, 1992.*

Kot, Greg. "On a Musical Limb." *The Chicago Tribune.* May 17, 1998.*

———. "Playing with Pain." *Chicago Tribune.* January 18, 1996.*

———. "Scarlet's Walk." RollingStone.com. October 29, 2002.

La Gorce, Tammy. "An Interview with Tori Amos." Amazon.com.

Lambeck, Silke. "Portrait: Tori Amos." *Brigitte.* July 24, 1996.*

Lane, Harriet. "My Husband and I." *The Observer* (UK). January 5, 2003.*

Lanham, Tom. "Ramble On." *The Wave.* March 9–22, 2005.*

———. "Tori Amos: Scattered Shots." *Paste.* February/March 2005.

Laue, Christine. "Finding that Uncomfort Zone." *Omaha World Herald*. March 20, 2003.*

Laxton, Beck. "Flaky Pastry." *Keyboard*. April 1996.

Legaspi, Althea. "The Gospel According to Tori." *Illinois Entertainer*. March 2005.*

Levy, Adam. "Side Orders." *Guitar Player*. July 1998.*

Levy, Doug. "Tori Amos on Midwinter Graces, Family Connections, and the Birth of Light." flavorwire.com. November 25, 2009.

Llewellyn Smith, Julia. "I Needed a Child in My Life More Than I Knew." *Daily Telegraph*. September 5, 2001.*

Lobley, Katrina. "What's the Delay Here?" *Sydney Morning Herald*. May 6, 2005.*

Long, April. "On the Couch: Tori Amos." *NME*. May 1998.

Lynskey, Dorian. "33 Things You Should Know About Tori Amos." *Blender*. November 2002.*

Lynskey, Dorian. "Reasons to Be Tearful." *The Guardian*. February 11, 2005.*

Macias, Chris. "One for the Road." *Sacramento Bee*. April 11, 2003.*

Malins, Steve. "Tori Amos: 'I'm the Queen of the Nerds.'" *Vox*. May 1994.*

Marin, Maya. "liveDaily Interview: Tori Amos." livedaily.com. June 4, 2009.

Martin, Richard. "Voices in Her Head." *Willamette Week*. September 9, 1998.*

"Marying the Marys." *Rocky Mountain Bullhorn*. September 1, 2005.*

Mattera, Adam. "Tori Amos." *Attitude*. May 1998.*

Mazur, Matt. "Abnormally Attracted to Sin: Tori Amos Talks with PopMatters." Popmatters.com. May 22, 2009.

McCollum, Brian. "The Time Tori Amos Is Bringing a Band to Detroit." *Detroit Free Press*. April 28, 1998.

McDonnell, Evelyn. "Tori Amos — Boys for Pele." *Rolling Stone*. January 23, 1996.

McLennan, Scott. "Tori Amos: Roses and Thorns." *Rip It Up*. April 28, 2005.*

McPherson, Douglas. "Tori Amos." *Keyboard Player*. June 2009.

Meinert, Kendra. "Getting Inside Tori's head." *Green Bay Press-Gazette*. March 20, 2003.*

Merriman, Chris. "Listen with Mother." *Get Rhythm*. October 2001.*

Mervis, Scott. "Music Preview: Tori Amos Takes a 'Walk' Through America." *Pittsburgh Post-Gazette*. March 14, 2003.*

Micallef, Ken. "With a New Double Album Up Her Sleeve, Tori Amos Confesses All." *Pulse*. November 1999.*

Michelson, Noah. "Songs in the Key of Sin." *Out* via undented.com. May 5, 2009.

Middleton, Fraser. "American Odyssey." *Glasgow Evening Times* (UK). December 19, 2002.*

Miers, Jeff. "On the Road Again." *Buffalo News*. March 14, 2003.*

Min, Ben. "Tori Amos." *Elle*. March 2002.*

Montalbano, Liz. "Mystic Pieces." *Phoenix New Times*. September 24, 1998.*

Moon, Tom. "Tori Amos." *Philadelphia Inquirer*. May 3, 1998.*

Moran, Jonathon. "Tori Thinks We're the Bee's Knees." *Sunday Telegraph*. April 17, 2005.*

Morgan, Laura. "Tori Amos: Holding Hands with Violence." *Axcess*. February 1994.*

——. "When I Was 17: Tori Amos." *Seventeen*. November 2002.*

Morse, Steve. "Once Again, Tori Amos Finds Healing Through Music." *Boston Globe*. April 24, 1998.

——. "Tori Amos Play-Acts Pop's Images of Women." *The Boston Globe*. September 16, 2001.

——. "Tori Amos: Under the Volcano." *Boston Globe*. January 19, 1996.*

Mudd, Jonathan. "Who Is Tori Amos?" *BAM*. October 2, 1992.*

Mullins, Tommy. "Meeting the Muse: Tori Amos." *Music Monthly*. December 2001.*

Mundy, Chris. Interview with Tori Amos. *Rolling Stone*. November 1994.

Murphy, Peter. "The Hostess with the Gnosis." *Hot Press*. April 2005.*

Myers, Caren. "Famous Amos." *Details*. March 1994.*

"My First Time." *Boyz* (UK). October 12, 2002.*

Neal, Chris. "Tori Amos." *Performing Songwriter*. November 2006.*

Nelson, Steffie. "Personality Crisis." MTV.com. October 5, 2001.

Newman, Jeffrey L. "Tori Amos: Creme Puff with a Machete." *Between the Lines*. August 20, 1998.*

Nicholls, Mike. "Heart-to-heart." *What's On*. October 1991.*

Nichols, Natalie. "American Doll Posse." *Los Angeles Times*. April 29, 2007.

——. "For Amos, Passion Fuels 'Venus' Voyage." *Los Angeles Times*. September 23, 1999.

O'Brien, Lucy. "Pianosexual." *Diva*. February 1996.*

O'Horan, Kevin. "Sting Like a Butterfly." *Herald Tribune*. April 1, 2005.*

Oliveira, Daniel. "If a Piano Could Cry, Tori Amos Would Be Its Tears." *Best*. October 1999.*

Ollison, Rashod D. "Some Singers Write Their Music; Amos Researches Hers." *The Baltimore Sun*. August 21, 2003.*

Orloff, Brian. "Musings of a Musical Maverick." *St. Petersburg Times*. March 31, 2005.*

———. "Tori Amos' New American Journey." Neumu.net. November 7, 2002.*

———. "Tori Makes Sweet Honey." RollingStone.com. February 21, 2005.

Ouellette, Dan. "Amos Treks the U.S." *San Francisco Chronicle*. December 15, 2002.*

Painter, Chad. "Columbus Is a Spider Town." *The Other Newspaper*. August 14–20, 2003.*

Pantone, Gina. "Enigmatic Piano Prodigy Tangles with a Dangerous Insect Story." *Chicago Innerview*. April 2005.*

———. "Tori Amos." *Venuszine*. June 1, 2007.*

Paphides, Peter. "Ginger Nut." *Time Out*. December 20, 1995.

Pareles, Jon. "At Lunch with Tori Amos." *The New York Times*. April 23, 1998.

Parks, Wendy and Gitsels, Edwin. "Tori Amos, The Wild Minister's Daughter." *Hitkrant*. March 12–19, 1994.*

Peradotto, Nicole. "Famous Amos." *Buffalo News*. August 29, 1999.*

Peters, Stephen. "Launch Exclusive: Tori Amos." Launch.com. April 12, 2000.*

Picardie, Justine. "Kooky or What?" *London Independent*. January 16, 1994.*

Piltz, Albrecht. "Screams and Whispers." *Keyboards* (Germany). June 1992.*

Pines, Ethan. "Tori." *News & Record*. August 16, 1996.*

Planer, Lindsay. "It's Best to Catch Her Live." *Break*. August 14, 1996.*

Poitras, Helene. "Tori Amos." *Voir*. February 24, 2005.*

Powers, Ann. "Tori Amos." *New York Times*. January 14, 1996.

Pride, Dominic and Chuck Taylor. "Amos Bares Soul on Atlantic Set." *Billboard*. January 13, 1996.

Quantick, David. "In the Piano Room with Tori Amos." *Blender*. August/September 2001.

"Questionnaire: Tori Amos." *Q*. March 1996.*

Radner, Ronni. "Scarlet Fever." *Out*. November 2002.*

Rauh Solomon, Tracey. "On the Road to Healing." *The Citizen*. February 27, 2003.*

Reesman, Bryan. "Five Questions with . . . Tori Amos." *Keyboard*. May 1999.*

———. "Tori Amos and the Evolving Lives of Her Songs." *Goldmine*. May 7, 1999.*

Richina, Richard. "Tori Amos: A Musical Journey." *Insights*. Fall 2003.*

Riddle, Scott. "The Deeper You Listen." *Nuvo*. July 1994.*

Robertson, Jessica. "Tori Amos Straps on Her High Heels." AOL Music News. September 18, 2006.*

Robinson, Lisa. "Tori Amos Preaches to Girls in the Choir." *New York Post*. April 17, 1998.

———. "Tori Amos: One on One with Lisa Robinson." iGuide. January 1996.*

Robinson, Stephen. "Red Letter Day with Tori." *Hot Press*. November 20, 2002.*

Robjohns, Hugh. "Checking in with the Choirgirl." *Sound on Sound*. July 1998.*

———. "Mark Hawley: Recording Tori Amos." SoundonSound.com. July 1998.

Rodgers, Larry. "Amos Casts Critical Eye on America." *Arizona Republic*. December 15, 2002.*

Rooksby, Rikky. "Tori Amos." *Making Music*. January 1996.*

Rose, Greg. "Tori Amos: 'Music Is My Passion, It Really Is Magical.'" Virgin. com. October 30, 2009.

Rule, Greg. "Tori! Tori! Tori!" *Keyboard*. September 1992.

Russell, Stephen. "The Honey Trap." *The Big Issue*. June 2005.*

Ryan, Francesca. "Tori Amos." *She*. May 1998.

Sakamoto, John. "Tori Amos Talks About Her Miscarriage." *Jam*. March 24, 1998.

Salvato, Jennifer. "Passionate Singer/songwriter/performer Is the Volcanic Goddess of Pop . . ." *The Home News & Tribune*. September 27, 1996.*

Sandall, Robert. "The Keys to Success." *The Sunday Times*. January 16, 1994.*

Sandbloom, Gene. "What's So Amazing About Really Deep Thoughts." *The Network Forty Magazine*. July 1992.*

Scheerer, Mark. "Tori Amos Is the Coolest G-url on the Web." CNN.com. February 1, 1996.

Schlansky, Evan. "Q&A with Five Faces." *American Songwriter*. July 2007.

Sculley, Alan. "Amos Takes Listeners on Aural American Odyssey." *Florida Today*. November 8, 2002.*

———. "Tori Amos." *Music Monthly*. September 2005.*

———. "Tori Amos." *St. Louis Post Dispatch*. July 15, 1994.*

———. "Tori's Body Map." *Alameda Times-Star*. April 11, 2003.*

Sembos, Mike. "Pieces of Her." *Fairfield County Weekly*. March 31, 2005.*

Shapiro, Gregg. "Cover Girl." *Next*. September 7, 2001.*

Shaw, William. "Earth Angel." *Details*. August 1998.*

Sheats-Johnson, Jamie. "Scarlet's Walk Leads to NC." *Charlotte Observer*. February 21, 2003.*

Sheehan, Tom. "Her Life's Tori." *Melody Maker*. February 5, 1994.

Sheffield, Hazel. "Tori Amos Interview." hazelsheffield.blogspot.com. June 2009.

Silezi, Andrea. "A Girl and Her Piano." *Musica*. 1996.*

———. "Tori Amos: The Devil in a Cup of Tea." *Musica*. 1996.*

Simmons, Silvie. "Heart Shaped Box." *Request*. June 1998.*

———. "From Venus to Tori and Back." *Aloha*. November 1999.*

———. "Southern Upbringing — Tori Amos." *Rumba*. March 13, 1998.*

———. "Tori Amos." *Top*. December 1999/January 2000.*

Simonart, Serge. "The Devirginizing of Tori Amos." *Nieuwe Revu*. February 1994.*

Sinagra, Laura. "Larger Earthquakes." *Spin*. April 2005.

Smith, Aidan. "A New Tori Policy." *Scotland on Sunday*. February 20, 2005.*

Smith, Andy. "A Fervor Over Tori, One Way or Another." *The Record*. September 1, 1996.*

Smith, Chris. "Tori Amos." *Us*. July 1998.*

Smith, Christopher. "Tori Amos: The Loudest Voice in the Choir." *Performing Songwriter*. September/October 1998.*

Snow, Mat. "Can We Talk?" *Q*. February 1992.

Solomon, Evan. "Tori Amos." *Shift*. April 1996.*

"Songs of Praise." *Woman's Journal*. November 2001.*

Spera, Keith. "Tori, Tori, Tori." *The Times-Picayune*. October 30, 2001.*

Spoto Shattuck, Dianne. "Tori Amos." *Women Who Rock*. January/February 2004.

St. Leger, Marie Elsie. "Under the Pink." *Rolling Stone*. February 1, 1994.

"Star Challenge." *M* (UK). October 26, 2002.*

Stepanek, Martin Jan. "My interview with Tori 2009 + beautiful photos." martin-jan.typepad.com. May 9, 2009.

Stone, Sarah. "There's Something About Tori." *Red Direct*. September 2001.*

Stoneman, Justin. "World of the Strange." Virgin.net. September 11, 2001.*

Stovall, Natasha. "To Venus and Back." *Rolling Stone*. September 20, 1999.

Strange Little Girls press release. Atlantic Records online. July 2, 2001.

Struges, Fiona. "Tori Amos: 'Now I Can Open My Eyes.'" *The Independent*. October 27, 2006.*

Sullivan, James. "Tori Amos' Got a Ticket to Writhe at Filmore." *San Francisco Chronicle*. May 4, 1998.*

Swarbrick, Susan. "The Third Degree." *The Herald*. June 4, 2005.*

Takiff, Jonathan. "Amos' Piano Pop More Than Music." *Philadelphia Daily News*. March 24, 1994.*

Talkington, Amy. "SCENE: A few of Tori's favorite things." *Seventeen*. March 1996.*

"Talking with . . . Tori Amos: 'My Dinner with Clunky.'" *People Weekly*. February 5, 1996.*

Tarshis, Joan. "Tori Amos: Under the Pink." *Schwann Spectrum*. Spring 1994.*

Tate, Nick. "As Alter Ego Scarlet, Singer Holds Mirror to America on Tour." *Atlanta Journal-Constitution*. November 8, 2002.*

Taylor, Christian. "Tori Amos — Living Doll." samesame.com.au. April 29, 2007.*

Taylor, Chuck. "Atlantic's Amos Rerelease May Add Volume to Cut That's Been 'Silent All These Years.'" *Billboard*. March 29, 1997.

Taylor, Lewis. "Tori Amos Goes in Search of America." *The Register-Guard*. July 25, 2003.*

"Tea with the Waitress." *Record Collector*. November 1999.*

"Telephone interview by a reporter in Singapore." yessaid.com. January 23, 1996.

"The Beekeeper Is a Career Best for Amos." *Word*. April 2005.*

"The College Daze of Tori Amos." *Student Advantage Magazine*. Winter 1998.*

"The History Seen with Other Eyes." *Aftenposten*. March 14, 2005.*

"The Sense Impressionist." *Word*. February 2005.*

"The Story on Tori." *Philadelphia Daily News*. January 23, 1996.*

"The Tori Party." *Deluxe*. May 1998.*

"The Tori Story." *News and Observer*. August 11, 1996.*

Thompson, Jonathan. "Q: The Interview — Tori Amos." *Independent on Sunday*. November 16, 2003.*

Tierney, Eric J. "Tori's Sacred Journey." *Salt Lake Metro*. September 2005.*

Timmermans, Arjan. "Tori Amos: No Ordinary Girl." *Windy City Times*. June 8, 2005.*

Tood, Matthew. "Tori's Glory." *Attitude*. November 1999.*

"Tori Amos — Scarlet's Walk." *Entertainment Weekly*. September 20, 2002.

"Tori Amos Covers All the Bases." *Ice*. September 2001.

"Tori Amos Finishes New Disc." *Rolling Stone*. May 24, 2001.

"Tori Amos Tries to Explain Writing Process." Associated Press. March 23, 2005.

"Tori Amos: Grace, Feeling & Passion." *Visions* (Germany). September 1992.*

"Tori Amos: Interplanetary, Most Extraordinary." *Time-Off* (Australia). November 24–30, 1999.*

"Tori Amos' Musical Journey Across America." The Music Room, CNN.com. February 13, 2003.*

"Tori Amos: Quick in Progress." Q. March 2005.*

"Tori Amos: *Scarlet's Walk*." *Alternative Press*. October 2002.*

"Tori Amos." *Attitude*. September 2001.*

"Tori Amos." *ExBerliner*. February 2005.*

"Tori Amos." *Oor*. September 8, 2001.*

"Tori Amos." Q via thedent.com. January 2004.

"Tori Amos." Q. May 1996.*

"Tori Amos." *Rag*. May 2005.*

"Tori and Drugs." Q. May 1995.*

"Tori Makes Waves." *Next*. April 2, 1999.*

"Tori Traces a Journey." Associated Press. November 14, 2002.

Touré. "Tori Amos — The Power and the Passion." *Rolling Stone*. June 30, 1994.

Treacy, Christopher John. "Back to the Garden: Tori Amos Gets All Biblical on Her Latest." HartfordAdvocate.com. March 31, 2005.

Trombino, Cosette. "Silent All These Years." *Virtual Guitar*. October 1999.*

Turpin, Adrian. "I Hope You're Going to Make Me Out to Be Funny." *Scotland on Sunday*. November 16, 2003.*

Uhelszki, Jaan. "Tori Amos Echoes Voices of America." *The Mercury News*. April 11, 2003.*

Van de Kamp, Bert. "The Circus Girl." *Oor*. March 7, 1992.*

Van den Heuvel, Hans. "Tori Amos." *Oor*. May 7–21, 1994.

Van der Horst, Herman. "Sane or Insane." *Oor*. September 18, 1999.*

Van Looij, Annemarie. "The Beekeeper." *Oor*. March 2005.*

Van Melick, Ruud. "Tori Amos: Out of Her Mind." *Nieuwe Revu*. April 8, 1998.*

Varine, Pat. "Tori Amos." *The Duquesne Duke*. March 20, 2003.*

Varty, Alexander. "Tori Finds Her Inner Berserker." *The Calgary Straight*. September 3–10, 1998.*

Venable, Malcolm. "Music, Bees and the Bible." *The Virginian-Pilot*. August 11, 2005.*

Verna, Paul. "Tori Amos Isn't Alone in her Hotel." *Billboard*. April 4, 1998.

Voog, Ana. "Chat with Tori Amos." Anacam.com. October 20, 1999.*

Walters, Barry. "American Doll Posse." *Spin*. June 26, 2007.

Watson, Vaughn. "Scarlet's Walk." *Providence Journal*. November 14, 2002.*

Waugh, Bob. "Tori Amos." *WHFS Press*. Spring 1994.

Weiss, Murray. "The Story Behind 'Me and A Gun.'" iGuide. January 1996.*

Welzenbach, Michael. "Tunes by Torchlight." *The Washington Post*. July 20, 1984.

"What Do Tori Amos and Bette Midler Have in Common?" *New City*. September 1996.*

Whitney, Brooks. "What's the Story, Tori? Pleasing Herself Is the Key to Offbeat Singer's Success." *Chicago Tribune*. June 25, 1996.*

Wilde, Jon. "Conservatory Parties." *Melody Maker*. November 1991.*

Williams, Allison. "Tori Amos Interview." *Time Out Dubai*. July 6, 2009.

Williamson, Nigel. "A Bride Stripped Here." *The Times*. September 21, 1999.*

———. "Relative Values." *The Sunday Times Magazine*. May 24, 1998.

Willman, Chris. "Brazen. Precious. Poetic. Profane." *Los Angeles Times*. January 30, 1994.

———. "To Venus and Back." *Entertainment Weekly*. September 24, 1999.

Woodard, Josef. "Tori Amos: Little Earthquakes." RollingStone.com. April 2, 1992.

"Words Are Weapons — and Men Know that Very Well." *KulturSpiegel*. September 2001.*

Yackoboski, Chris. "Tori Amos: Roasting Men and Sweet Bikers." *What*. February 1996.*

Yadegaran, Jessica. "Tori Amos." *The Tribune*. April 11, 2003.*

Zaleski, Annie. "Tori Amos: Scarlet's Walk." *Alternative Press*. November 2002.

Zeidler, Thomas. "Strange Little Girl." *Action* (Austria). November 2001.*

Zonkel, Phillip. "Amos Puts Herself in 'Venus' Frame of Mind." *The Daily News of Los Angeles*. September 25, 1999.*

Zulaica, Don. "liveDaily Interview: Tori Amos." *liveDaily*. August 31, 2005.*

* accessed via yessaid.com.

ACKNOWLEDGMENTS

I would first and foremost like to thank ECW Press (specifically Jack David for taking the book on, my editor Crissy, and interns Jessica Rose and Tamara Chandon) along with the rest of the amazing staff for shepherding this book to publication. Thanks also to Marcel van Limbeek, Matt Chamberlain, Eric Rosse, and Joe Chiccarelli for the generous time you granted in interviews for this project. Thanks as well to the countless print and web publications that have followed Tori's career with such fantastic interviews and features, with specific thanks to the Tori Amos fansites — especially toriphoria.com, hereinmyhead .com, and yessaid.com — who do such an amazing job cataloging these articles for fans in the first place.

On a personal note, as always I would like to thank my parents, James and Christina-Thieme Brown, for continuing to tirelessly support my various artistic goings-on (both literary and musical); my brother Joshua T. Brown; to my angel Dena, I say a thank you for you every day; the extended Brown and Thieme Families; Alex Schuchard and Jackson Schuchard for being the coolest Godson in the world!; Andrew and Sarah McDermott; "The" Sean and Amy Fillinich; Adam

Perri; Chris "SEE" Ellauri; Matt, Eileen, and Kamelya Ellen Peitz; Richard (thanks for the past 10 years with Versailles), Lisa and Regan Kendrick; Paul and Helen WATTS!; Bob O'Brien and Cayenne Engel; Lexi "Clown" Federov; Rose Reiter and Gerry Plant; MVD Distribution/ Big Daddy Music; Aaron "Whippit" Harmon for continuing to have my back musically week in and out; Joe Viers/Sonic Lounge Studios for 10 years of great ears; Andrew Neice @ Melodic Rock; Keavin Wiggins @ Antimusic.com; Cheryl Hoahing at Metal Edge; Tim @ Brave Words/ Bloody Knuckles; Rock and Roll Report; John Lavallo and Take Out Marketing; Larry, Joel, James, and everyone at Arbor Books; Aaron, Gabriel, Victor, John, and everyone at SCB Distribution/Rock N Roll Books; Bookmasters; Jasmin St. Claire, thanks for hanging in there, we finally made it!; Lemmy Kilmister; Curt and Cris Kirkwood/ Dennis; Ben Ohmart/BearManor Media; Jack, Crissy, David, Simon et al at ECW Press; Tony (congrats on beating the big C!) and Yvonne Rose at Amber Books; Richard Anderson at Cherry Red Books; Jason Rothberg and Tracii Guns, thanks for the opportunity to be involved with telling this amazing story; Stephan Jenkins and Third Eye Blind for the opportunity to work on an In the Studio book with you!; and finally and without arrogance of any sort implied, thank you to the music fans who buy and read my books, and specifically this series, as you keep them coming!

Nashville-based music biographer **JAKE BROWN** has published 30 books, including In the Studio titles on AC/DC, Tom Waits, Heart, Prince, Rick Rubin, Red Hot Chili Peppers, Mötley Crüe, Alice in Chains, Motörhead, Meat Puppets, Third Eye Blind, Dr. Dre, and Tupac. He's also the author of *Suge Knight: The Rise, Fall and Rise of Death Row Records, 50 Cent: No Holds Barred, Biggie Smalls: Ready to Die,* and titles on Kanye West, R. Kelly, Jay-Z, and the Black Eyed Peas. Brown is also the co-author of Tracii Guns' memoir, a featured author in *Memoirs of Rick James: Confessions of a Super Freak,* and the co-author of retired adult film star Jasmin St. Claire's *What the Hell Was I Thinking?!*

Brown has appeared on Fuse and Bloomberg TV, and his work has received additional press in publications like *USA Today,* the *New York Post, Vibe, Billboard, Revolver, Publishers Weekly* and on NPR and MTV.com, among many others. Brown was recently nominated alongside Lemmy Kilmister for the 2010 Association for Recorded Sound Collections Awards in the category of Excellence in Historical Recorded Sound Research. Brown is also the owner of the hard-rock label Versailles Records, distributed nationally by Big Daddy Music/MVD Distribution.